JACK BARTH

A FIRESIDE BOOK

PUBLISHED BY SIMON & SCHUSTER INC.

NEW YORK LONDON TORONTO SYDNEY TOKYO SINGAPORE

AMERICAN

Quest

Fireside
Simon & Schuster Building
Rockefeller Center
1230 Avenue of the Americas
New York, New York 10020

Designed by Chris Welch
Manufactured in the United States of America

10 9 8 7 6 5 4 3 2 1

Library of Congress Cataloging in Publication Data
Barth, Jack.
    American quest/Jack Barth.
        p.   cm.
    "A fireside book."
    1. United States—Description and travel—1981–
—Humor.   2. Barth, Jack—Journeys—United States—
Humor.   I. Title.
E169.04.B37   1990
917.304′92—dc20   90-33570
                                                                    CIP

ISBN 0-671-68240-7

"More *Easy Rider*" and "Life in a Multiplex" first appeared in
Premiere magazine.
"Kissing Ten TV Sirens of the 1960s" first appeared in *Film
Comment* magazine.
"*Please Stand By*" and "The Freddie Prinze Commemorative
Stamp" first reported in *Spy* magazine.
Coca-Cola is a registered trademark of The Coca-Cola Company.
Permission for reproduction of materials granted by the company.
Pogo the Clown and other Gacy art reprinted with permission.
Maps by Bill Shortridge.

Special Thanks
Don Baker
Dolores, Grace, Randolph and Sue Barth
Matthew Bialler
Lester Erwin
Doris, Rebecca and Stanley Fellerman
Peter Fonda
John Wayne Gacy
Stuart Gottesman
Bruce Handy
Harlan Jacobson
Howard Karren
Steve Kessler
Doug and Susan King Kirby
Richard Kuehndorf
Sylvia Kuehndorf
Paul Lewis
Nancy Lundquist
Susan Lyne
John Margolies
Joe Mastrianni
Brian McCoskey
Carolyn McGirt
Bill McNeill
Susan Morrison
Roger Nunley
Heywood Robillard
Alan Schafer
Ed Silver
Gavin Smith
Ken Smith
Amy Treend

Extra Special Thanks
Julie Kuehndorf
Trey Ellis
Michael Carlisle

No Thanks at All
Dennis Hopper
Jack Nicholson
Maria Kalligeros/National Car Rental
Julie Newmar and her minion
Pat Wexler and Lynda Friendly/Cineplex Odeon
Richard Nunis/Disney World

Editor
Jeff Neuman

Ultra Megaspecial "Creative" Consultant
Mike Wilkins

In Memoriam
Tim McGinnis, Patron Saint of Cool Books

Contents

Introduction: You Be the Reader

hen people ask what I'm working on I always say, "Nothing." This reply is quick and simple and not aggressively impolite, and for some reason people usually laugh, though it's not really much of a conversation starter. If, however, they ask, "What's this *American Quest* thing all about?" I sometimes make an effort to explain.

I am never able to formulate a punchy syllabus, however. I futilely try to pinpoint a common literary touchstone, or assert that it will be like nothing ever written before. But I just *know* that after my rambling, inarticulate mumbling, the other person is wondering how I expect to write 70,000 words when I have *no idea* what I am talking about. So I usually fall back on the short answer: "Who cares? Shut up."

But they haven't bought this book, as you have. So here goes:

What if Charles Kuralt had a nervous breakdown—sorry, I mean "an epiphany"—and realized that the way to discover America was not by cruising around with three sweaty men in an RV, videotaping sunsets and perversely glorifying things the real America no longer needs, but by accepting us at face value and documenting things we really care about?

Or:

What if George Plimpton, instead of writing about what it's like to be a geeky author posing as an inferior athlete—ha ha, professional football players sure are bigger and better than I am, ha ha—did things like work at McDonald's or try to kiss TV stars?

And what if, instead of being some basso profundo network wheat licker or some popcorn-pushing Ivy League patrician, they were me? *That* is *American Quest.*

I begin by drawing up a list of twenty things I would like to do. Most involve driving somewhere and doing something. Some can be performed without leaving my desk (except to go to the bathroom). What they have in common is that each reflects the wants, the profoundest desires of a middle-class American born in the 1950s or '60s.

These are not heroic feats; they are common deeds that many normal people perform every day. The difference is that I will attempt twenty different such actions, for no good reason other than to get behind the scenes and learn more about the institutions that have influenced me. No doubt, I'm going to meet resistance from those who don't understand why they should be nice and let me do this, and I'm going to have trouble convincing them. That should be fun!

Before I present my *American Quest* shopping list, here are some examples of other people's quests as reported in *USA Today*, the only paper that lets you know how North American baseball players are faring in Japan:

➤ Ronald Regan, of Rockaway, New Jersey, the owner of a chain of weight-control centers, has spent $20,000 trying to meet his famous "namesake." "What started out as a curiosity became a challenge," he says. "I couldn't understand why someone couldn't meet the President." His efforts have included sending telegrams to every member of Congress and kissing Rex, the Reagans' dog.

➤ Before Elane Sollins died, she asked that her ashes be scattered at third base in Baltimore's Memorial Stadium. Charles Kalus is pursuing his mom's wish. "She was a big Orioles fan for years," he says, "and third base is where her darling Brooksie [Robinson] played."

The difference between these quests and my own is that mine will be sagaciously devised in the hopes of ascertaining some homely truths about this grand old land, and then maybe getting mentioned in *USA Today*, whereas they just wanted to get mentioned in *USA Today*. I'll do a few cross-country quests, where the driving is both the means and the end, others for which driving will be simply a means to an end, some where driving will be an ends to a mean, and the rest where driving will be neither means nor end, just something that other people are doing while life passes me by.

I have a special relationship with cars. I don't own one, but I spend about six weeks a year driving cross-country, either in rentals or driveaways. So each time I find myself behind the wheel, I am on my way—in a hurry—to someplace new and exciting, unlike most people in cars, who are on their way to work. It's kind of like Sunday night TV: when you had to get up the next day and go to school, watching, say, "The Ed Sullivan Show" wasn't nearly so spectacular as it should have been. But now that you're out of school, Sunday night is pure viewing enjoym . . . bad example.

America needs a spokesperson for the highway nomads of the 1990s, someone willing to accept a few modern realities without mourning for a way of life that even Kerouac outlived. William Least Heat Moon, author of the landmark road tome *Blue Highways*, snivels that every time he gets on an interstate, it's like his hippie van is being sucked along and he has no control—he forgets he has a steering wheel, brakes, and an accelerator. He wants to be a road guy, but only if he can do it as some sort of eagle spirit or something, firewalking across the good earth on his precious back roads. To me, this is like saying you'd be willing to play professional baseball, but only if the pitchers would *stop throwing so fast*. Big Chief Moon's the kind of guy who drives 55 in the passing lane with his turn signal blinking away for miles.

Too many "on the road" reporters feel inclined to talk to people, to get the feelings of the "common man." I don't go for that stuff. What for? The common man in Cody, Wyoming, is thinking about the same R-rated movie that the common man in St. Augustine, Florida, rented last night. This book will not be encumbered with quotation marks.

I hope after reading this you will want to do your own questing. As rude and suspicious as the populace is now, just imagine how sublimely nasty folks would be if there were *thousands* of Americans out there pursuing demented visions! But do you have what it takes? Can you answer "Yes" to any of the following questions?:

1) When I've finally arrived at my destination, do I immediately want to be going someplace else?
2) Have I forgotten the details of every book I've ever read, but recall distinctly the "Love, American Style" episode in which Bert Convy takes a pal to see an exotic dancer whom he describes as "Filet—rrrrrrrrraw!"?
3) Do I save the empty wrappers of test-marketed snack foods that failed, because I think they'll be worth something some day?
4) While some people who get stuck with lemons make lemonade, when I break my glasses do I try to make contact lenses?
5) Don't I just hate those new coffee cans that have only eleven ounces instead of sixteen, but cost the same? I mean, who are they fooling, huh?

If you answered "Yes" to any of the above, then you've probably "got what it takes" to do your own questing, and if you're still with me, here are my quests:

1) Re-create the journey of the characters in the movie *Easy Rider* with the stars of that film: Peter Fonda, Jack Nicholson, and Dennis Hopper.
2) Help search for Bigfoot in Washington State with a university professor who plans to hunt the man-beast by helicopter and kill it.

3) Initiate a paint-pellet-gun war among bratty kids in a giant shopping mall in Bloomington, Minnesota.
4) Milk a cow in Iowa.
5) Drive a monster truck over a Japanese auto in Idaho's rugged Aryan-survivalist country.
6) Dress as a hippie and try to get kicked out of Disney World.
7) Visit all the graves of the 1927 Yankees' so-called Murderers Row lineup.
8) Plant a fake news item in a major national publication.
9) Work for a week at the world's largest McDonald's, in Vinita, Oklahoma.
10) Figure out the coolest places to drive in America, then go to them.
11) Get *Guinness Book of World Records* murderer John Wayne Gacy to paint the cover for *American Quest*.
12) Sit in on drums with Iron Butterfly in concert playing "In-A-Gadda-Da-Vida."
13) Make a list of ten TV-star women I want to kiss, then try to kiss them.
14) Make a list of ten Great Americans whose hands I want to shake, then try to shake them.
15) Travel for a week with no-money-down instant-real-estate-millionaire guru Dave Del Dotto.
16) Play the great miniature golf courses of America.
17) Work for a week manning the Frito-Lay hot line.
18) Try to get a stamp issued by the postal service honoring Freddie Prinze.
19) Work for a week at the most typical multiplex movie theater in America.
20) Spend a week just hanging out in Breezewood, Pennsylvania, which bills itself as the Town of Motels.

That's about it; wind me up and away I go. One final word about procedure, out of fairness to those who were willing to participate in *American Quest*. None of the questees had any knowledge of my other quests, except for what I wanted to tell them. All they knew was that it was "for a book." In other words, the corporations that were open-minded enough to allow me a firsthand view of their inner workings had no idea they'd be appearing in the same book as John Wayne Gacy's skull clown, and if you try to draw any connection between them you have Silly Putty for brains.

★ ☆ ★ ☆ ★ ☆ ★ ☆ ★ ☆ ★ ☆ ★ ☆ ★ ☆ ★ ☆ ★ ☆ ★

How to Tell If You Are Having Fun

INTRODUCING THE QUEST QUOTIENT

It wouldn't be right to create a fun new activity without also devising some quantitative means of determining precisely how much enjoyment it is actually providing. Otherwise, what would be the point? Therefore, in the spirit of a team of distinguished professors (from "Gilligan's Island" and "Nanny and the Professor"), doctors (Howard, Fine and Howard), and mentalists—slash—nightclub performers (The Amazing Kreskin, Uri "Spoons" Geller), I have programmed the world's most sophisticated computer—the human brain, although it doesn't have a slot for Nintendo cartridges—to input and evaluate all the factors that go into a quest, churn those numbers around, and figuratively spit out a so-called "rational" number that can be used for purposes of comparison.

But not so fast. When did you ever read a treatise that just gave away the pertinent equation without forcing you to make at least an effort to understand the thought processes behind it? (Or at least forcing you to figure out how far ahead to skip?) Why, that would be like tickling someone's baby without having gone through the horribly excruciating (*believe you me*, or so I hear) pains of labor! Forget it. No coochie-coochie-coo till you contemplate the following paragraphs.

The first component of my formula is the sum of all the things that make a quest worth attempting. A well-conceived quest contains several basic elements; the more abundant those elements, the better the quest:

➤ A quest should involve travel: the more miles, the better. Driving mileage (M_d), the standard to which all other factors in the Quest Quotient are compared (kind of like how you get frequent-flyer mileage when you rent a car—I mean, how is that "worth" a certain number of miles? It simply *is*. Look, just keep on skimming), is ten times more respectable than flying mileage (M_f).

➤ A quest almost always requires preproduction, in the form of phone calls and letters. It seems reasonable to consider letter writing to be twice as arduous as telephoning. Empirical research reveals that one phone call (**P**) levies a stress equal to ten miles of driving (car phones count double); thus, each letter (**L**) written is the equivalent of twenty miles of driving.

➤ I suggest the quest entail a bit of romantic titillation, or at least the false, empty promise of some. Because any actual success in this arena must be amply rewarded, each instance of "intimacy" (**I**) should be worth the equivalent of a solid day's driving, about one thousand miles. Since I have a girlfriend (as of this writing) who will read this—Hi, Julie! Uh, how d'ya like it so far?—I shall limit this category to "pretty girls pecked on the cheek," but you can call it whatever you like.

➤ Your quest need not make everybody happy: after all, think how dull newspapers, movies, and books would be without conflict. Conflict is what makes a quest worth doing. Anyone can accomplish something if nobody is there to wish he would drop dead (**D**) or at least stop phoning. This number should include people who were mean to you in the performance of your quest as well as people who *will be* mean to you when they find out about it. Each person who wishes you would blow up and dry away is the equivalent of one hundred miles of driving.

➤ Finally, your time (**T**) is worth something, although if you're like me that "something" is more indefinable than, say, *money*. Each day you completely devote to the quest (or traveling to the site of the quest) is worth one hundred miles.

This sum is then compounded by the Difficulty-Aggravation multiplier (**DA**). No matter how far you drive, how many calls and letters you make, et cetera, a quest isn't worth its sodium chloride if:

a) it seems at all possible you might be able to accomplish it, or
b) its execution doesn't cause you frustration beyond even that of trying to get through to the service department of your local cable TV monopoly.

The Difficulty-Aggravation (**DA**) multiplier, a subjective rating on a scale of 0 to 10, is a way of severely weighting the Quest Quotient so as to favor quests that seem hopeless at the outset *and* are utter misery to perform. A 10, for example, would have to be something like "creating a lasting world peace" by "standing nose-deep in a leech-infested septic tank," or maybe "winning the lottery" by "standing in line for a lottery ticket." A 0, on the other hand, would be something like "not going to work" by "staying in bed" or "getting people to like me" by "keeping my mouth shut."

Finally comes the denominator—a penalty for screwing up, for corrupting yourself with the two things a proper quest should avoid: failure (**F**), expressed as the percentage of incompletion, and expense (**$**), in dollars.

Okay, now you can peek at the formula. Have fun!

$$QQ = \frac{(M_d/100 + M_f/1000 + P/10 + L/5 + (I \times 10) + D + T) \times DA}{(F/10) + (\$/100) + 1}$$

Just for the sake of word count, let's try a few examples. Say you're a dashing Midwestern archeologist and you decide to search for a lost ark. It's probably in the Middle East or somewhere, so you'll need to fly about ten thousand miles, then drive another thousand. You're a man or woman of action, not words, so you make only, say, five phone calls and write two letters. You get to kiss one pretty girl (or neat guy) along the way, you get about fifty Nazis mad at you, and the whole *sh-boom* takes fourteen days. Raiding a lost ark is a tall order, with a high Anticipated Difficulty factor; it also turns out to be death-defying and dangerous. Give it a **DA** multiplier of 9. You find the ark, so your incompletion percentage is 0, and it all costs about $45 million.

$$QQ = \frac{(1000/100 + 10,000/1000 + 5/10 + 2/5 + (1 \times 10) + 50 + 14) \times 9}{(0/10) + (45,000,000/100) + 1}$$

Now, you might have found this quest very exciting, but your Quest Quotient is a dreadful .002. *This was an unsuccessful quest.* Had it not cost so darn much, you would have scored much higher. Compare this to something more low-key. Let's say you live in Colorado, and you like this movie actress—*really* like her. It seems to you she would probably get a big kick out of it if you would shoot the President. After writing a few (148) fan letters and attempting a few (89) times to phone the actress, you drive for three days to get to Washington, D.C. (1,950 miles). You squeeze off a couple of rounds before four mean secret-service agents jump you and cause you much aggravation. The President suffers wounds over only 30 percent of his body and recovers. The actress is so impressed she gives you a big, smoochy kiss. Many American citizens (twenty-seven, including two of the secret-service agents) are outraged by your actions, which cost you a total of $248 for gas, postage, long-distance phone, and ammunition. You get a **DA** multiplier of 6: only a moderately difficult task, but a bit inconvenient.

$$QQ = \frac{(1950/100 + 0/1000 + 89/10 + 148/5 + (1 \times 10) + 27 + 3) \times 6}{(70/10) + (248/100) + 1}$$

Congratulations! You've scored a commendable 56.1! See what you can accomplish by keeping expenses down? Anyway, this should help you keep the Quest Quotient in its proper perspective. As I have demonstrated, it is *very, very, very important*.

Do not be confused by your "gut feeling" about your quests. Numbers don't lie; you do. The quest quotients in this book range from 31.2 down to 7.8, with most in the 10-to-20 range. Here's how to rate your own:

Over 30
Nirvana: An extremely well-conceived and -executed quest confronting obstacles galore.
20–30
Shangri-La: A successful quest in which you fulfill a lifetime desire or die trying.
15–20
San Francisco: A solid workmanlike effort. Maybe you didn't drive far enough.
10–15
Chicago: A good idea. Maybe you think you had fun, but deficient in several departments. Try adding a twist next time.
5–10
Newark: Something went wrong somewhere. Your quest wasn't questy enough.
1–5
Detroit: It was a dumb idea, it was too simple, and you spent too much money.
Under 1
France: A dismal failure. Bad everything. You should have seen it coming.

ROAD HOGS . . .

More Easy Rider

Twenty years before this book, the story of a different quest, Easy Rider, directed by Dennis Hopper, produced by Peter Fonda, and starring the duo, wowed the topless in crowd at Cannes and won the coveted

International Film Prize from the International Interchurch Film Center, which stated, "This film expresses with authentic emotion, through the bewilderment and wildness of today's youth, the search for a sense of life and the search for God in a world without pity."

I, of course, am not of the *Easy Rider* generation. President Bush himself has praised me and my peers for our lack of bewilderment and wildness, for having become instead "a *Dirty Harry* generation." (Do you feel lucky, punk? Blam-blam! Ahhahahaha!) As a twelve-year-old at the time of *Easy Rider*'s release, the only "searching" I did was for lost whiffle balls, but still, to me, the film's thrilling portrayal of freedom as an open road and a teardrop gas tank full of cash and Hi-Test was more than a passive experience. In fact, with the possible exception of *Goldfinger*, *Easy Rider* was probably my most potent cinematic influence. I have vivid memories (and Super-8 films) of popping wheelies on my Schwinn Sting-Ray while digging the *Easy Rider* soundtrack on my Kenner Close 'n Play and squeezing my Tigeroo—grrrrr . . . grrrrrrrr! I might never get to search for America with a pal on a Harley, I figured, but hey, man, freedom is just another word for liberty, and who wants to end up like those guys anyway?

Yeah, who wants to end up like *them*?

Columbia Pictures billed the film as "a drama about a man who went searching for America and was unable to find it." Apparently, America was hungry to view itself as diseased and demented in the eyes of a rich, Hollywood proto–Brat Pack. The film, which cost a little over $500,000, grossed over $60 million, of which Fonda, who two years ago made *Mercenary Fighters*—no comment—in South Africa, reportedly owned 22 percent. This windfall led to some uncool feelings: Hopper was unhappy with his percentage.

Perhaps it is this bitterness over finances that has quashed all attempts at a sequel. Comedy writer Michael (Tony Orlando with Steel Spikes in His Eyes) O'Donoghue worked on an aborted sci-fi epic about the bikers in heaven after a nuclear holocaust. George Segal, Richard Benjamin, and Dan Greenburg shot an unreleased spoof, *Alfred Rider*, about a man who went looking for Southampton and couldn't find it. Ho ho ho!

For twenty years, us *Easy Rider* fans have been left hanging. Hopper, now back on the Hollywood A-list, is too busy for *Easy Rider II*. Fonda's cinematic dance card is also full; besides busting the

South African cultural boycott, he remains the Olivier of the cable-ready action flick.

And that's why I have to take it upon myself, along with a road pal, Trey Ellis, a postmodern novelist, to provide a sequel of sorts. From Los Angeles to New Orleans and beyond—me dressed in fringed-suede "Billywear" and Trey bearing Captain America's stars and stripes upon his back—we'll see if this great big old land of ours has changed.

Unfortunately, we'll have to forget about re-creating their journey by motorcycle; nobody will rent a one-way chopper from L.A. to Florida, and we can't afford to buy motorcycles and go through the costly hassles of registration and insurance. Besides, there are all these helmet laws now, and I already went out and bought a Dennis Hopper hat. Also, we invited Jack Nicholson to come along (see letter), and let's face it, at his age he's probably not up to a long motorcycle trip. He never actually responded to the letter, probably because he figured it was, as my postmodern writer pal Trey would say, a *fait accompli.*

We contact National Car Rental about the possibility of some kind of promotion (something like this: "Yay! National sure is the way to go!") in exchange for a loan of one of their fabulous classic convertibles, so at least we might go in vintage style. Incredibly, they like the idea, and it looks like we will get an early-'60s T-Bird. Yay! National sure is the way to go!

However, the car lady drags her feet on the specifics, and *the afternoon before we are due to leave for L.A.*, she backs out. I am set to throttle her; *she has torpedoed a quest and must perish.* She patiently abides my rant: "The original idea for the story was how great National is," I lie. "Now the title of the story is 'Fuck National,' " I lie again, possibly. She commences sobbing, upset. I try to calm her down, like it's *my* ineptitude that caused this. She is undeserving of sympathy but inconsolable and thus escapes my further wrath. I phone Trey.

"I think it's time for some Good Cop, Bad Cop," I say. "You are the Good Cop." He calls the car lady; she is truly afraid of me, informing Trey that I am a crazy lunatic. He smooths her ruffled feathers (figuratively, as far as I know): we won't get a car to drive cross-country, but we'll at least get a free National classic for use in L.A. while we're cooling our heels waiting for a driveaway agency to secure us a car to Florida. Even so, the car lady still doubts my stability: " 'Fuck National,' he said, 'Fuck National,' " she says, in numb disbelief—and probably suspects I will guide her car over a cliff or drive it to Florida anyway.

Grrr . . . grrrr. I try to refocus on the quest and regain my Eye of the Tigeroo. Tomorrow we'll be fetching Nicholson at his reclusive Mulholland Drive (Beverly Hills!) pad. Will we flip off rednecks in a pickup? Will we find a pitiless world? Who knows? You can't plan these things. After all, searching for America and not finding it— that's a tall order.

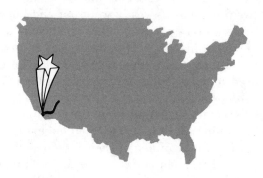

We fly into LAX, onto a runway similar to that near which our heroes consummated the drug sale to Phil Spector that netted them the nest egg they stashed in their gas tanks before leaving for Mardi Gras, then retirement in Florida. Los Angeles will be dreamy—an exciting meeting with Hopper himself, a quick swing up to Nicholson's Beverly Hills (!) pad—then we'll speed off on our transcontinental adventure.

We arrive shortly after dawn at Hopper's Venice digs, knowing he is very busy editing his latest film, *Backtrack*. (He ignored my calls and letters, but you know artists—it's cool.) Maybe he finished cutting the film last night and will stagger outside his heavily architected sheet-metaled shed and say, "Hey, man, come on in for some coffee —or 'tea'—while I put out some extra food for the Gila monster and dust off my bedroll before we hit the road."

Not knowing where his Bloods and Crips pals from *Colors* might be lurking, we stay in the car and honk the horn in time to the opening guitar chords of "Born to Be Wild": Honk-honk Honkhonk Honkhonk Ho-ho-honk/Honk Honkhonk Honkhonk Ho-ho-honk. . . .

He never shows. One of my original hopes was to get a photo of Fonda and Hopper, looking paunchy and old, waving goodbye to us sleek youngsters as we head out on the highway. I spoke to Fonda once—he gave me some info on locations they used—but he wouldn't give me his phone number, promising he would call again, collect, " 'cause I'm not gettin' anything outa this." He never called again; a great photo opportunity up in smoke, and now I probably have no chance with his foxy daughter Bridget.

Well, at least we'll be cruising America with Jack Nicholson, and that will really be something. We head to his hilly hacienda. Jack sure has a fine place, we imagine, since all that is visible from the road is a big gate. From our letter, he knows we're coming, but he never emerges. (Later we are told he is in a foreign land shooting *Batman*.) What a letdown, but definitely the last one. A driveaway company has found us a Cadillac Eldorado to deliver to a certain Madame Tinker-toy (not her real name) in Boca Raton, Florida. *"Getcher motor runnin'/Head out on that highway. . . ."*

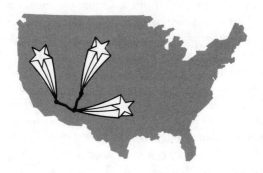

In *Easy Rider*, Madame Tinkertoy's House of Blue Lights was the New Orleans brothel George Hanson (Nicholson) extolled to Captain America and Billy shortly before rednecks performed baseball-bat lobotomy on him in the bayou. At the bordello our heroes dropped acid with two harlots, Mary (Toni "Mickey" Basil) and Karen (Karen Black). Since prostitution is illegal in Louisiana, we decide to do our chores in Nevada.

In Vega$, our first stop, Trey enthusiastically makes a beeline for the Yellow Pages to check under Brothels and Whorehouses, but none are listed. Then, under Nightclubs, he finds a place called Scandalous.

"Hi, are you a brothel?"

"We're a nightclub, and every night a lot of lovely single ladies come here who love to party."

Despite Trey's prurient zealousness to make the ninety-minute trek out to the "nightclub" (whorehouses are not allowed in Las Vegas proper; they might prove a bad influence on the slot guidos), we chicken out—our first and definitely last compromise. We opt instead for passive entertainment, *Crazy Girls: Ecstasy de Paris*. Thirteen topless cuties wearing Kaiser helmets can-can onstage to the theme from "Hogan's Heroes." Look, it was either this or *Nudes on Ice*.

The next morning finds us winding over Hoover (*Lost in America*) Dam en route to Valentine, Arizona, site of the ranch where Captain America fixed a flat in the background while a rancher symbolically reshod a horse in the foreground. We snoop around a ranch that resembles the location, until dogs chase us back into the Caddy. Nearby, in Truxton, we meet Ray Barker at his Frontier Cafe and Motel. Sure, he remembers them coming to shoot on the Collins ranch, now the Hunt ranch. Yes, he saw the film, but he didn't much care for it, or any movies or TV, for that matter. "I'd rather tromp around in the hills," he says, Sam Shepard–like. He looks outside to admire our motorcycles. "Uh, nice Eldorado," he says.

We follow the route of the filmmakers through spectacular Monument Valley. Traveling shots of the choppers cutting through the great American Southwest were filmed here. Monument Valley is not an overprotected national park but rather a Navajo reservation, so you can veer off-road and carve your own path to unspoiled natural beauty. I particularly recommend the Mexican Hat rock formation if you're not driving your own vehicle.

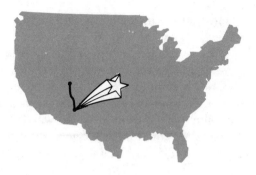

Art-gallery-laden Taos, New Mexico, has become a refuge for the peyote-popping remnants of the *Easy Rider* generation. At least a half-dozen people connected with the film or the filmmakers have moved here since. Approaching from the west, you pass the site of the movie's opening scene, the drug deal that was supposed to have taken place in Mexico. The commune the boys visited is based on the nearby New Buffalo Commune (the scenes were actually filmed near Malibu). Somewhere in neighboring Questa are the hot springs where our heroes skinny-dipped with two comely communards to the tune of the Byrds' gripping "I Wasn't Born to Follow," co-written by Carole King ("And if you think I'm ready/You may lead me to the chasm/ Where the rivers of our visions/Flow into one another. . . .").

Clearing away heaping plates of blue-corn pancakes that tasted like syrup-covered plaster, our waitress in the tony Taos Inn directs us to the hot springs. An hour later Madame Tinkertoy's Eldorado finds itself once again taxing its suspension as we bounce over ruts and chaparral down (we will later discover) the wrong path. The chassis barely clears the ground, but complacent Trey refuses my entreaties to park the car and walk; he treats this "suggestion" as if I'd just asked him if I could borrow his toothbrush to scrape away a few stray dingleberries. After bottoming out in a gulch, the Caddy's rear wheels spitting plumes of New Mexico brown, Trey concedes, with Captain America–like magnanimity, that this might be a mistake, and we somehow manage enough traction to turn around and head back to town. The belly-scuffed car's now making a strange hum and emitting a nagging burning smell, but none of the idiot lights on the dashboard are flashing. We proceed.

In the old Taos jail (it was set in The Lone Star Beer State in the movie, but the filmmakers had heard too many Texas redneck horror stories), Captain America and Billy met hung-over ACLU lawyer

George Hanson and ignited Jack Nicholson's acting career. At the county jail, we meet officer Fabian Mascareñas, thirty, who looks more like Erik Estrada than our image of the Taos lawman: Dennis Weaver's McCloud. Son of a biker and owner of three Harleys himself, Mascareñas knows Hopper well. "I arrested him once; we all did." Today, though, Hopper is to Taos what Janis Joplin is to Port Arthur, Texas, or John Wayne Gacy is to Norwood Park, Illinois—a rascally favorite son. Parts of Hopper's *Backtrack* were filmed here. "What kind of Harleys you riding?" Officer Mascareñas asks. But it's time to move on.

A young Chicano prisoner in Day-Glo orange pajamas asks Trey, "How are you doin'?"

"Fine," says Trey. "You?"

"Doin' time, man, doin' time."

Trey's bombshell reply: "Aren't we all?" The convict squinches his nose in a "Who cut the ched'?" manner and hustles back inside.

Trey insists that this dialogue be reported as an example of something, of his fool habit of interacting with people on the road. I contend it is pointless, that one can have a perfectly good time on a trip without chatting up convicts.

The old jail, where they filmed the movie, is now—you guessed it—an art gallery. Bryans Gallery, run by Michael McCormick, a friend of Mrs. Fonda's, now stocks the two cells with expensive Southwestern art. To the side hangs an unofficial historic marker about *Easy Rider* and stills from the movie—the only tangible recognition of the film we would find throughout the entire trip.

We cruise-control on a Sunday morning through deserted Texas at 85 m.p.h. until I'm pulled over in Snyder by an extremely pleasant Chicano trooper, who issues only a warning. Tomorrow we'll reach the ultimate *Easy Rider* mecca: Morganza, Louisiana, the setting for the memorable scene at Mrs. Blackey's Diner, the beating death of Jack Nicholson, and the final shotgun blast.

We stop first in Lottie, Louisiana, home of R. O. Long's service station, reportedly a frequent hangout of David C. Billodeau, who played the pickup truck's trigger man. ("Want me to blow your brains out?" and "Why don't you get a haircut?" are his two immortal lines.) He isn't in. "Probably out scouring Saint Landry and Pointe Coupee parishes for more day-player work," jokes Trey.

"Too bad. You could have *talked* to him," I say with a sneer.

We were told Mrs. Blackey's has stills from the film on its historic walls. We find it abandoned and padlocked. The Cat Man, so identi-fied in the credits for the Cat Diesel Power cap he sports in the diner scene (a fashion statement that soon thereafter would sweep the land), rounds up as much of the cast as he can and meets us at Mrs. Blackey's successor, Jimmy's Quick-Stop. We enter and immediately face the CAT MAN (Hayward Robillard) and CUSTOMER #4 (Paul Guedry), both in their sixties. A black man with an American flag on his back and a mutton-chopped Jewboy in fringe jacket and cowboy hat—New Yorkers, retracing the steps of two California trust-fund hippies who, twenty years ago, ridiculed them to the world.

DEPUTY
What the hell is this? Troublemakers?

CAT MAN
You name it, and I'll throw a rock at it, Sheriff.

"I told Jack Nicholson I'd beat him within an inch of his life if he made the South look bad," the charismatic Robillard tells us, un-prompted. "The biggest disappointment in my life was Jack Nichol-son."

Robillard is a self-described "coonass" (native Cajun); his ad-libs (and maybe Nicholson's, but we'll never know because he didn't come along like he promised) were what propelled *Easy Rider* to cult status and record-breaking B.O. "Just say whatever comes into your mind as we walk in," Hopper had directed.

DEPUTY (Sheriff Arnold Hess, Jr.) enters Jimmy's under the same white cowboy hat he wore in the film. Back then, he was Dean Martin to the Cat Man's Jerry Lewis.

CAT MAN
Check that joker with the long hair.

DEPUTY
(o.s.)
I checked him already. Looks like we might have to bring him up to the
"Hilton" before it's all over.

CAT MAN
Ha! I think she's cute.

DEPUTY
Isn't she, though. I guess we'd put him in the women's cell, don't you
reckon?

CAT MAN
Oh, I think we ought to put 'em in a cage and charge a little admission
to see 'em.

GEORGE [*Nicholson*]
(sighs)
Those are what is known as "country witticisms."

Robillard says he was originally asked to be in the film because
the filmmakers were having union trouble and wanted him to in-
tercede. After spending three days in Morganza, the crew recognized
Robillard's potential and urged the Cat Man to come to Hollywood
and become a character actor. "I'd have loved to have been able to
try for a year or two," says Robillard. But he had three-quarters paid
off some new construction equipment, so he couldn't go. Throughout
the filming, Robillard had been eying Hopper's leather jacket; it
would be great for deer hunting, his passion. Hopper said he'd mail it
to him as soon as they finished shooting cover shots back in L.A. Says
Robillard, "That lying bastard never did."
    The men in the cafe, minus the Deputy (as a lawman he didn't
think it would look right), participated in the moonlight pummeling
of Nicholson. During one take, the foam pad inside Nicholson's sleep-
ing bag slipped; he took a hard whomp on the leg from Mr. Guedry
and exploded out of the bag, screaming. Mr. Guedry chuckles at the
memory.

One of the teenage girls who ogles the three drifters in the cafe was dietician Rose LeBlanc Moore, now thirty-seven. She's not happy with the way her acting debut turned out. "It didn't do justice to the South," she says. "I don't know what they were trying to prove." She swears, with absolute sincerity, that when a crew member invited her and her statutorily underage friends back to the hotel in Baton Rouge for a "pot party," she declined by saying, "My parents have enough Tupperware." Years later she read an interview with Fonda in which he said the girls in the film were probably still sitting there drinking soda. "You can tell Peter Fonda I'm happy sitting in Mrs. Blackey's drinking Coke," she says. "It's better than the other kind."

As Trey would say, the little girl has grown up.

We follow Mr. Robillard to his home for a tour of his pigs, rabbits, chickens, and hunting dogs. He feeds us "pork cracklin," a home-made fried pork rind de-lite. A neighbor cruises by with some tooth-achily sweet pralines—such hospitality a contrast indeed with their filmic personas. Robillard tells us that it's funny, but just a few weeks earlier another writer, Michael Medved, had come to spend some time with him for a book *he* is doing. As a writer hoping for something exclusive, this is funny to me only if they dumped Medved in a bayou.

Robillard tells us that soon after the dope-smoking Los Angeleno crew had wrapped this location and cleared out of town, he learned of their propositioning the criminally youthful girls. If he had known earlier, he says, "I wouldn't say we would have killed them, but they wouldn't of been in a condition to leave."

We are reminded of a scene early in the film, one which we will not re-create. The boys are pulling into a motel after a long day on the dusty trail. They bounce toward the office on their growling steeds, revving their fine motors and beeping their horns. The propri-etor comes out. "Hey, you got a room?" shouts Captain A. above the racket. They gun their engines to show what outstanding guests they will be. VRROOM VROOOOM!! "Hey, man! You gotta room?" The little man retreats into the office and illumines the NO VACANCY sign. Billy, stunned that the man found it so "easy to be hard," gently proffers "the finger."

We are also reminded that *Easy Rider* was promoted as being "90 percent ad-libbed." However, it is becoming apparent that Fonda, Hopper, and co-writer Terry Southern had preconceived a pitiless America of savage rednecks—and were dead set on projecting that vision. We call it entrapment; but as the Cat Man might say, if you're huntin' for gators, don't use your legs as bait.

Like the bikers, we drive on to New Orleans, but instead of LSD, we pop antihistamines and wander around the voodooey St. Louis Cemetery No. 1. On the corner of Bourbon and Toulouse, where Madame Tinkertoy's is supposed to be, we ask a hot dog vendor how to find the legendary brothel. He doesn't know. *He doesn't know!*

On to our apocalypse. On to . . . Disney World. You see, we've heard hippies used to be banned from here; would we finally meet those malevolent Dixie possum-pluggers that *Easy Rider* tells us infest the heartland? Trey slings on a Hendrixian Afro wig, a red-white-and-blue headband, and a provocatively militant Fishbone T-shirt to force things a bit. However, we are generally ignored. Trey does encounter a barricade at the entrance to Frontierland's awesome roller coaster, Thunder Mountain.

"It's closed for a week," says an employee.

"But I'll be back in New York then," Trey whines.

"What a shame."

I hand-roll a Bugler tobacco doobie decoy and we toke in front of Cinderella's castle, daring rebuke from The Man. Visitors gape, but no squadron of electric-golf-cart-driving, walkie-talkie-toting security Nazis shows up. I shoot Super-8 film of us "getting high," but it is of no avail. Either times have changed, or the fabled Disney "perfect world" is just, as Mike Schmidt would say, *a big lie.* I will send an angry letter to the head of Disney World when I get back to New York (see Angry Letter).

That night, as Trey guides the Caddy through Hobe Sound, on the posh outskirts of Palm Beach, a red-and-blue bubble light goes off behind us. Immediately Trey pulls over, extracts his license and the car's registration, and gingerly steps out. Luckily he no longer sports that "I-thought-he-had-a-knife" wig, just that shocking T-shirt. He calmly explains the driveaway-car particulars as the red-and-blue lights dance over him.

"I've got a bad feeling something's not right," says the bovine cop.

Have I remembered to mention that Trey is an African American? And that we are near Palm Beach (maybe Trump Beach by the time this is published)?

"Sir," says Trey, "would you like me to explain?" Trey recounts the journey thus far, including, no doubt, his ultrawitty exchange with the prisoner in Taos. . . .

"Why aren't you on motorcycles?" the cop asks.

Although our *Easy Rider* re-creation would be that much more cool if we were assassinated by graft-swollen police on a dimly lit access road, the cop begrudgingly dismisses us, and Madame Tinkertoy's Caddy gobbles white lines and asphalt, hellbent for Boca Raton.

HAPPY LETTER #1 . . .

Dear Mr. Nicholson

Dear Mr. Nicholson:
Or should we call you Jack, because we're sure that after two weeks of cruisin' the American Southwest, we'll all be not only on a first—name basis but also pals for life? Starting November 1, we'll be re—creating the route immortalized by you and your two zany partners in crime, Dennis "Billy" Hopper and Peter "Captain America" Fonda, in the movie that made you all legends, Easy Rider. We'll set out from the Big Apple to personally pick you up at your home in the Big El Lay and fly the highways to the Big Easy and then, as a special bonus, onward to the Big Orange (Miami). And hold on to your helmet——all expenses paid!!!

　　We know what you're thinking: "Who would want to get their brain respattered all over the Louisiana bayou by a gang of rednecks?" Well, you know what they say: "If you fall off a horse . . ."

　　We'll pick you up around 2 P.M. on the 1st. We're looking forward to meeting you; we're big fans of all your movies (except Heartburn).

See ya then,

Jack Barth and Trey Ellis

P.S. You wouldn't have an old cooler you wouldn't mind bringing, would you?
P.P.S. Go Lakers!

Dear Disney

Mr. Richard Nunis
President
Walt Disney World
Lake Buena Vista, FL 32830

Dear Mr. Nunis:

I am writing to you because I saw you on a TV commercial for AT&T and you seem like a caring person. I am a divorced father of two: Jennifer, age nine, and John, Jr. (known as Spunky), age five. Last month (November 10), I took advantage of the Veterans Day holiday to take Jennifer and Spunky to Disney World. Their mom thought I was spoiling them, and maybe I was——tough.

Anyway, we were having a great time, enjoying ourselves among the other family-oriented visitors there, when we happened to see a couple of, for lack of a better word, hippies. I have nothing against people for the way they dress or the way they act, as long as it doesn't disturb anyone else. But these two, one a black guy and the other a Caucasian male, were so outlandish that they were causing quite a stir. The black guy had on what had to be a huge "Afro" wig——nobody's hair looks like that, nobody's. The other guy looked like Dennis Hopper in Easy Rider——very grubby. It seemed like they were out to "prove something," only what I do not know. I've enclosed a photo to prove my point.

Anyway, we tried to ignore them, but they were so boisterous——perhaps they are on drugs, I naturally thought. The kids were amused by them, so I shrugged it off and went about our day. But when we got to the Kodak photo spot near Cinderella's Castle, there they were again. Only this time they were passing a hand-rolled cigarette——a "joint." This was just too much. I looked around for a security guard, or at least an employee to get a security guard, but could find nobody handy. I rushed the children out of there, but the damage was done.

After I returned to New York, I got a call from my ex-wife. It seems the kids told her all about the "hippies" and their behavior. If this wasn't bad enough, Jennifer has been caught pretending to "smoke a joint" in her room. Naturally, I caught all heck for this, and, while nothing's definite yet, my ex-wife is talking about reducing my visitation rights because of this.

Normally I would just chalk this up to "the modern world." After all, you can't raise kids in a vacuum. On the other hand, you do try to shield them as long as possible. My complaint is

that Disney World should be the one place where kids can be
shielded from such abnormal behavior. If a security guard had
"busted" those foul hippies for what they'd done, my kids
might have learned a valuable lesson. Better yet, why don't
you keep people like that out of the Magic Kingdom in the first
place? Didn't you used to have rules about the way people
dressed——their hair, their clothes, their smell? I don't
know why they'd want to come to such a nice place in the first
place, but this being a free country I should be free to avoid
looking at such filth when I'm at Disney World, for gosh
sakes.

Could you please clarify what your rules are for behavior
at Disney World? I would really like to know why nothing was
done to prevent those two from ruining my vacation.

Sincerely,

Jack Barth

☆ ☆ ☆ ☆ ☆ ☆ ☆ ☆ ☆ ☆ ☆ ☆ ☆ ☆ ☆ ☆ ☆ ☆

Sorry, Bridget...

"EASY WHINER"

An exciting real-life scene from the offstage drama that was the making of *Easy Rider*, as recalled by residents of Morganza, Louisiana. (All dialogue guaranteed authentic to the best of their recollections of twenty years ago.)

INT: ROAD HOUSE: LATE AFTERNOON

Atavistic Cajun caterwauling rumbles distortedly from a jukebox. The room is dark, dingy, and smoky. A handful of LOCALS, men and women, warped-skulled progeny of inbreeding and ignorance whose tongues loll and flicker senselessly from misshapen oral cavities guarded by rotted-out dental husks, HOOT GIBBERISH in ungrammatical bursts.

CAPTAIN AMERICA, Old Glory rippling across his jacket with each flex of his impressive lats, talks on the pay phone, plugging his exposed ear with an index finger in an attempt to hear the other party over the insane shouting. GRUBBY LOCAL #1 sizes him up suspiciously; GRUBBY LOCAL #2 glares malevolently, rubbing the large revolver stuffed into the waist of his girth-stretched jeans.

                    CAPTAIN AMERICA
          (shouting testily into receiver)
          I said Caddy! And it's got to be air-con-
          f*cking-ditioned. You have <u>heard</u> of air
          conditioning——this <u>is</u> 1968, at least where
          I come from, in civili-goddamn-zation.

GRUBBY LOCAL #1 taps CAPTAIN AMERICA on the shoulder with a greasy paw.

                    GRUBBY LOCAL #1
          S'cuse me, Mr. Fonda, but please watch your
          language. There are ladies present, and
          around these parts we show some respect for
          the womenfolk.

CAPTAIN AMERICA
(to GRUBBY LOCAL #1)
"Around these parts," brothers shtup their
sisters, so get outta my face, motherf*cker.
Do you know who I—?
(suddenly, to car person on phone)
What?! There's not one godf*cking a.c.—ed
Caddy in Baton Rouge? Do you know who I am?
(pause, then he wilts a bit)
Uh, no. Actually I'm his son . . .

GRUBBY LOCAL #2 then butts in:

GRUBBY LOCAL #2
Gee, Mr. Fonda, Homer did ask you nicely
to tone it down a bit.

CAPTAIN AMERICA
Homer can s*ck my big famous Hollywood
movie star d*ck!

GRUBBY LOCAL #2 whips the revolver out of his girth-
stretched pants waist, c*cks it, and holds it to the left
temple of a startled CAPTAIN AMERICA.

GRUBBY LOCAL #2
Hang up, get out . . . or die.

★══════════════════════★══════════════════════★

COMPUTATION OF QUEST QUOTIENT

$$QQ = \frac{(M_d/100 + M_f/1000 + P/10 + L/5 + (I \times 10) + D + T) \times DA}{(F/10) + (\$/100) + 1}$$

Mileage driven: $M_d = 3500$
Mileage flown: $M_f = 4000$
Phone calls: $P = 37$
Letters: $L = 5$
Intimacies: $I = 0$
Drop Dead factor: $D = 4$
Days spent: $T = 12$

Difficulty-Aggravation multiplier: $DA = 7$

Failure rate: $F = 10$
Cost: $\$ = 1800$

QUEST QUOTIENT = 20.9

☞ *Analysis:*

Let the quests begin! Off to the races right out of the gate, with a mighty 20.9! This QQ demonstrates the value of balance: respectable scores in almost every category (except Intimacies, and then only 'cause of misplaced Vega$ prudishness). . . . DA a push-me, pull-you compromise between maddening intransigence of big-city button-pushers at outset and genial hospitality of road encounters; a theme that shall reverberate throughout, if you ask someone like me who's peeked ahead.

Kissing Ten TV Sirens of the 1960s

I am very excited about this one. I am composing a list of my ten favorite TV sirens of the 1960s, the women who taught me the true meaning of femininity and who (except for Lassie) awakened in me a stirring that hasn't yet

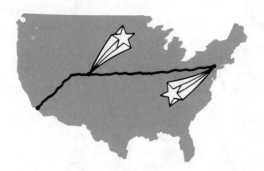

subsided (except for brief intervals), thank G⸫sh. I am going to see how many of the winsome tensome, without my pulling any "strings" or exploiting anything that would differentiate me from an average fan, are willing to let me kiss them. All I'll say is, "It's for a book."

Of all the quests I have set out to perform, this is both the most stimulating and the least promising. There's no way to compare the sense of accomplishment I might feel assembling McDLTs or scooping up sticky garbage from the floor of a multiplex with the rousing tremor of actually docking lips to cheek with one of my all-time favorite TV dolls.

On the other hand, it is immeasurably less frustrating to negotiate a bureaucracy of obliging and efficient corporate intermediaries than it is to deal with the stonewall snobbery and withering contempt of Hollywood agents and managers. While corporate America, at its best, comprehends the value of a smooth, buffed image of assured competence, and is typically willing to accommodate journalists in exchange for what passes for a fair shake, Hollywood's professional recalcitrants skirmish unabashedly for quid pro quo: why should I help you, they say—or, rather, their assistants say, if you can get through at all—if it doesn't help me?

One must obey the pecking order: if you want something from somebody, your chances of getting it are inversely proportional to his or her level of clout. If I were setting out to smooch all the Enumclaw, Washington, Daughters of the American Revolution, I would send a nice note directly to their chairperson, she would promptly respond, letting me know what would be convenient for them, and I would drive out there and pucker up. Done. If, however, I were instead trying to entice the lovelyish Princess Di into a wanton weekend in Elko, Nevada, her publicist probably wouldn't even return my calls, not even if it were for an all-expenses-paid *Ladies' Home Journal* cover story.

This quest, I figure, falls somewhere in between. The women I am soliciting have probably passed the prime of their careers; they are still young, still beautiful, and as talented as ever, but a hit TV show comes along—if you are very, very lucky—once, maybe twice but hardly ever, in a lifetime. The star-making apparatus has devoured these delectable honeys, and unless any of them are fortunate enough to have an agent or manager who has not only retained his industry stature over the intervening decades but also has enough class not to have dumped them, they are now employing middle-grade middlemen. Because of this, I am hopeful of getting through to at least *a few* of my quarry. And then only if they and their contact persons have a—shudder—sense of humor.

I draw up my dream list of '60s *femmes fantastiques*, trying to ignore secondary considerations, such as recent media ascension, that will surely have an impact on their availability. After delightful consideration, I've decided that if I could kiss any ten TV gals from the '60s, they would be (alphabetically):

Barbi Benton
Donna Douglas
Barbara Eden
Eva Gabor
Lassie
Tina Louise
Lee Meriwether
Elizabeth Montgomery
Julie Newmar
Karen Valentine

Winnowing my heartthrobs was not easy. Certainly Barbara Feldon, Joey Heatherton, Eve Plumb, and Stefanie Powers could have made any man's list. (Except maybe Joey—she scares me. When I tried to get a contact person for the luscious, leggy star of "Dean Martin Presents the Golddiggers"—a saucy venture bringing Vega$-style entertainment to our living rooms—I was given the name of an attorney, civil-rights fanatic hyphen Constitution abuser William Kunstler, a man who won't rest until the world is safe for mad-dog cop killers. I wouldn't want my heirs having to battle the savvy counselor over Joey's constitutional right to forget that an author was going to meet her at a club where she always hangs out and kiss her as part of a book he's writing so she accidentally hatchets him into nugget-size bits and wipes the handle clean of fingerprints.)

I send off a batch of what I hope are nonpsychotic letters to the ladies on my list. Weeks later, I have received no response. Several have switched or dropped their agencies recently, and I can uncover no forwarding address. Meanwhile, out in L.A., as if the trickiness of this quest needed exacerbating, a crazed young lunatic "fan" has stalked and shot dead a cute young actress, Rebecca Schaeffer. Thanks a lot, Mr. Double-Y Chromosome. Now, more gingerly than ever, I must track them down, one by one, find new ways of approaching them, get them to appreciate my quest, set a time and place, and —smaaaaaaaaack!!!

What follows are profiles of my individual pursuits of each of these alluring shemales: a gallery of fantasy beyond the imagination. . . .

BARBI BENTON

Background: Barbi has a two-pronged appeal: not only did she appear as a fetching country cutie on "Hee Haw" (which technically began in the '60s, although Barbi didn't join until 1971), but also, in the '60s, she had been the fantasy gal for every boy's fantasy guy —Hef. I must admit, when I first saw "Hee Haw"—despite its bouncy "Laugh-In" format—I found it unbearable, especially when they went to a song by those goony twins. Barbi made it palatable, but only now do I realize what a great show it was (and is), and that

Roy Clark and Buck Owens are not two hick fools, but highly re-spected, rich as shit, country music giants.

Quest: I write to Barbi's agent, at Joshua Gray & Associates in L.A. I follow up and reach a snooty guy who says he hasn't seen my letter but is willing to pronounce, "It doesn't sound like something she'd be particularly interested in." Will this quest even get out of the proverbial starter's gate?

Obviously the man has no insight into Ms. Benton's mind, be-cause the next day I get a call from Barbi's social secretary, the helpful Penny Godoy, who tells me Barbi is amenable, and is awaiting my lips. The catch is, she and her husband are at their Aspen, Colo-rado, home (they have a pad in L.A. too), and I'll need to do it there. Penny reminds me that Barbi is a trained photographer, so I'd better know what I'm doing.

A few weeks later, I discover I have a frequent-flyer ticket that's expiring within days: I book a flight to Denver in the hopes of driving on to Smoochville. Unfortunately, Barbi and hubby are out of the country. I spend a pleasant few days in Colorado, visiting a motel in Monte Vista where you can watch movies from the drive-in next door while lying in bed; checking out the world's largest bug, in Colorado Springs; and grokking the awesome Mesa Verde cliff dwellings (hip-pies try to sleep in them and soak up the "energy," but they get bounced by the rangers), then return home to plot anew.

I decide to drive cross-country with my road pal Ken to Los An-geles, stopping in Aspen along the way. Crossing the continental divide just east of the beatific resort town, with a sinus headache causing an industrial hum that makes my brain feel like it's scraping against my cranium and oozing tissue like a slug on a sidewalk, I gather through the radio's static that the Cubs are hanging onto a slim lead in the late innings of the fifth game of their playoff against San Francisco.

We pull over in downtown Aspen, which is as claustrophobia-inducing and overbuilt as a horizontal public housing project, to catch the last few innings. Police are everywhere, guarding the fit, well-tanned (though not *that* tan, if you know what I mean) citizen-droids. What do they all do? Oh, that's right—they're rich.

The Cubbies blow it as dreaded, and my mood darkens. We phone our pal Mike in San Francisco to discuss our return trip, on which he will accompany us. But as he gloats demonically over the Cubs' tragic loss, he mentions in passing that he will be unable to join us; his bank-merger duties must take precedence. I'm not exactly having an Up with People kind of day—not the best time for me to be meeting one of the most desirable women in America.

We arrive at Barbi's home in the hills above town. We search for the entrance to this funky domain, and are admitted by Roberto, the houseboy. We meet Barbi's mister, a hyperactive real estate–monger. He orders us to go away and return in an hour: somehow my appointment had been mistransmitted.

You know that nasty throbbing you get somewhere between your nose and forehead just before an accident, that palpable sense of impending doom? Well, that feeling is creeping over me, superseding even a sinus headache.

We drive down the mountain and sit. An hour later, we return. And guess what? Barbi is fantastic. We were told she needed the extra hour to don makeup, but it is clear that she is a natural beauty. We chat amiably while her husband barks commands over the phone to a lawyer. Sunlight is fading, so we soon begin the session.

Since Barbi is the first of the sirens to pose, I'm not sure how stiff and formal the shots will be. But she clears that up fast, striking a perfect, cartoonishly animated expression that changes every shot. Me, I look like a dork.

Afterward, only with coaxing, Barbi modestly tells us about her "Learn to Play Piano in 30 Minutes" project, which has resulted in a successful album for her, with another on the way. She takes us to her workroom, where she unveils a secret entrepreneurial venture that reflects her sense of humor; it looks like a winner. Ahh . . . I am sorry, reader, if I have lapsed into hyperbole. I promise to get mean again real soon.

DONNA DOUGLAS

Background: Even if Louisiana's Donna Douglas never acts again, her portrayal of Elly May Clampett will go down in TV history as one of the most ingenious characterizations ever: charm and beauty mixed with lots of potential for humorous situations. If she had a flaw, it was that none of her suitors, from Dash Riprock to Sonny Drysdale (Louis Nye), were nearly good enough for her. In 1966, midway through her "Beverly Hillbillies" stint, Donna costarred with Elvis in *Frankie and Johnny*; the two supposedly became close due to a common interest in matters spiritual.

Donna loves critters, just like Elly May; she's currently marketing a line of dog-and-cat perfumes. Her personality is best summed up by a "Love, American Style" episode in which her boyfriend gets jealous when she lets a hunky neighbor stay with her while his apartment is being painted. Of course, an embarrassing mixup results, but the bottom line is, she truly is a *niiice* girl, and her boyfriend should have had more faith in her.

Quest: The phone number I am given for Donna is not that of an agent or a service, but of a friend. This makes it tricky to do any serious wheedling. Fortunately, she returns my call. Unfortunately, she phones out of politeness, nothing more. But the door is still open, I sense, as she attempts to sniff me out. She wants to know what sort of person I am, whether this will be a "quality" story. "I was offered one of the nighttime soaps," she tells me. "It would have shot me straight to the top, gotten me back on TV. But I turned it down."

She says she works with kids, so she mustn't lose her credibility;

she needs to know what kind of person I am, my morals, et cetera. I get the feeling she wants to know if I am a Christian, but is too genteel to come out and ask. All in all, she's an extremely nice person, particularly for a gorgeous actress from a monster-hit sitcom. It's sad that her career hasn't gone anywhere since "Hillbillies," if indeed that's what she wanted, but she seems to be, I don't know, what do they say in H'wood?—"centered."

She's leaving town; she says she might consider talking to me again upon her return. I am left with hope. The following month, while crossing the country, L.A. bound, I phone and learn that Donna will be in town when I arrive. But she never calls. I return home, lips still a'thirstin'.

BARBARA EDEN

Background: It took me a long time to appreciate the exotic charms of foreign beauties and women without "traditional good looks." For a long time, my ideal woman was—and still is, though I'm now more open to suggestion—Barbara "Jeannie" Eden: blond hair, blue eyes, great smile. . . .

Jeannie's got a new hit TV show, "A Brand New Life," and is once again riding the crest of the airwaves. This could spell trouble on the accessibility front. Of course, Jeannie never really left. She's made an *oeuvre* and a half of TV movies and quasifeatures over the past twenty years, including "The Feminist and the Fuzz" (opposite "fuzz" David Hartman; *Quest*-hater Julie Newmar played a hooker), "Let's Switch" (as a housewife who switches places with Barbara

Feldon, a feminist magazine editor), *Chattanooga Choo Choo* (with Joe Namath), and *Harper Valley PTA*.

Fun Fact: The "I Dream of Jeannie" TV-movie reprise, which starred Trapper John (from "M*A*S*H," not the old fat one), was directed by William Asher, who, interestingly enough, was married to questee Elizabeth Montgomery during her "Bewitched" heyday.

Quest: I reach Barbara's manager, Frances Byrne, at the L.A. firm of Hanson & Schwam. She's nice, but wants me to get a few confirmations of other kisses before taking it to Barbara. I call back a few weeks later with some names that look promising. Frances tells me she is leaving the company and will turn over the file to somebody else. Ullp! Do not pass go, et cetera.

While en route to L.A. I phone Barbara's publicist, Michelle Bega, and explain my quest. She's never heard of me, but, surprisingly, returns my call and lets me down easy. She explains that Barbara will be out of town when I am in L.A. and is incredibly busy to boot. Perhaps sensing the nature of this story, she wants to make it clear that she is turning me down for scheduling reasons, not because she doesn't like the idea or anything. I have to hand it to her: she's the only publicist or agent I encounter who has any sense of where I'm "coming from."

EVA GABOR

Background: Eva was born in Budapest in the 1920s, though the exact year is a matter of doubt. (She insists it was earlier than her biographers claim. Ha ha, just kidding.) Eva and her sister Zsa Zsa simultaneously appeared in my media consciousness, and, even though Eva was interested in being a serious actress while Zsa Zsa was more interested in divorcing seriously wealthy men, I must admit that, until "Green Acres," I lumped them together. Even as a child I wondered, "What do these women *do?*"

In 1965, "Green Acres" hit the air and Zsa Zsa was yesterday's goulash. Eva, even though she was older than my mother, knew how to push the right buttons on a youngster. Unlike Lucy, Eva, as Lisa Douglas, could be funny without hamming it up or cracking up at her own hilariousness. Most recently, she's been running Gabor International, the world's largest wig company. Clearly she's got quite a head under those wigs of hers.

Quest: Soon after I send a letter to Eva's manager, I get a call from her publicist at Rogers & Cowan. The publicist wants to know who the other women are. "I'll get back to you," she says after receiving this information.

I call back several weeks later. "I don't know, she has a very busy schedule," I am told. It's one of those conversations in which I'm supposed to respond, without sarcasm, "Well, thanks anyway. I deeply appreciate all the consideration you have given this." I do not sign off in this way, hoping to "leave the door open," but it is clearly a dead issue. Eva has been romantically linked with Merv Griffin, who has all these casino pals; the last thing I want is a visit from a Merv Goon, so I back off.

MERV GOON
Say, I think it might be a dandy idea if you laid off this Eva Gabor thing
right now, or else I'll have to break your darn leg.

ME
Okay.

MERV GOON
Aww, that's swell.

LASSIE

Background: I have to admit right off the bat that a crucial piece of Lassie trivia seems to have been driven out of the parking lot of my mind—the fact that every dog that ever played Lassie was a male. By the time this fact was recollected, my letter was on its way. I kind of feel like that guy who went steady with M. Butterfly.

Quest: Heck, I kiss my dog Spunky all the time, and he's all boy, so what's the big deal? And the reply is quick and encouraging. I get a call just four days later from a woman at the company that is producing the new "Lassie" show. She thinks it's a good idea and will contact Lassie's publicist, who will check with Lassie's trainer and call me. The trainer is Bob Weatherwax, son of Rudd, who trained Lassie during his-her heyday. This Lassie is a seventh-generation descendant of the original collie.

I don't hear from the publicist, so I call several weeks later. "First off," he informs me, "I should tell you that Lassie is and always has been a male."

"I [gulp] know. It's okay."

"Secondly, Bob Weatherwax is very protective of Lassie and what Lassie does."

"Can you ask him?"

A few days later he calls back to say, "They're being very protective of Lassie now; they're turning down a lot of stuff."

Everybody wants to kiss Lassie, I guess. Maybe another writer has beaten me to the punch. I lick my wounds—because I *can*—and move on.

TINA LOUISE

Background: If I had my pick of all the '60s TV gals, I'd probably want Elly May for my girlfriend, Samantha for my mom, Eva Gabor for my mom's best friend, Barbi Benton for my sister, Lassie for my dog, Lee Meriwether for my teacher, Karen Valentine for my babysitter and Jeannie for my housekeeper. But for a hot date at a drive-in movie, my choice would have to be "Gilligan's Island" 's Ginger Grant—Tina Louise.

Tina seems to suffer from a sexist, male-imposed double-whammy. She's worshipped as a red hot mama sex symbol, but at the same time is denigrated—thanks to a complicated series of defense mechanisms us guys have worked out that prevent a superattractive woman from becoming three-dimensional and thus unfantasizable and threatening—for a presumed lack of talent and intelligence. (Tina also has great tits.)

Tina has played in many movies over the years, from *God's Little Acre* to *O.C. and Stiggs*. A role that stands out in my mind, though hazily, is an episode of "Love, American Style" in which two guys duel over her. The normal, American guy picks an obscure weapon when challenged by the pompous foreigner (Cesar Romero?): a moo foy, which turns out to be some kind of Chinese cannon. The European guy agrees, thinking he said "new foils," which is understandable, right? I can't remember the ending, but I bet she ends up with the wimpy American.

Quest: A quick response: a friend of hers calls to say she'll do it! I just have to phone when ready. This news keeps me going for at least a month: no matter what happens, no matter how miserably I am treated, *I am going to kiss Tina Louise!* I phone a week before I hit L.A. Her service tells me she is back East until further notice. Waah.

When I return home, I immediately phone the number I've been given, which I assume is that of a service. But when a throaty voice asks who's calling, I realize I am *parlez-vous*-ing with Tina herself—in the flesh! The news, however, is not good. She says she is trying to audition for theater roles and is "not into having my picture taken for this right now."

"Right now"? Meaning today? This week?

Nope. "Right now" means forever, because there is no opportunity afforded for a follow-up. She is firm but pleasant, and I let it go. Another example of how I'll push hard at a publicist or manager who won't even present my quest, but won't bug a star once she's fielded the idea. Nonetheless, it's weird talking to someone who has no real good reason to decline except she just doesn't want to do it, and to hear her make some excuse that's supposed to make some kind of sense but makes none at all. Oh, well: at least she had the *common decency*—now there's an oxymoron for you—to respond.

LEE MERIWETHER

Background: Forget "Barnaby Jones": that was just two great actors who did a lot better in the '60s. And forget "Batman": Lee Meriwether, slinky as she may be, never measured up as Catwoman to either Julie Newmar or Eartha Kitt—and I've never heard a solid explanation why they kept changing actresses, either. What you're left with is "Time Tunnel," a 1966–67 show that featured Lee as Dr. Ann MacGregor, a brainy gal who wore a lab coat and pushed buttons fretfully. To all us Science Fair also-rans, *this* was pulchritude.

Quest: Oh, yeah, *that's* why they call it the Drop Dead factor. I write to Lee via her agent, who files my letter under NEVER RECEIVED. "She's out of town" is his first response, forgetting that I am, too. "She's really busy with 'The Munsters.' Call back later." Like after you've retired, *pal?*

ELIZABETH MONTGOMERY

Background: I have to admit, I was never too turned on by Samantha. She was so . . . domestic. Besides, how could any guy want to identify with Dick York or Dick Sargent? But recently I caught her in an old "Untouchables" episode as the cool, sexy Rusty Heller (surreally, Larry Tate appears in the same episode as a slimy sugar daddy) and began to see her appeal. Her father is the actor Robert Montgomery.

Rhetorical sidebar: Were you as shocked as I was when you saw *Citizen Kane* in your first Cinema Studies class and there was Endora? Did it ruin it for you, too?

Quest: As Samantha would say: "We-e-e-a-ll. . . . " I contact Samantha's manager, Barry Krost, and speak to Charles Dabney, his assistant, who seems like an okay guy. He promises to call back. After that, a void. A big, empty, telephone bell–less, FAX-less, "He's in a meeting can I take a message" void.

JULIE NEWMAR

Background: Julie Newmar, five feet ten, played a perfect robot on "My Living Doll" in the mid-'60s. She attained international celebrity and lionization as the original Catwoman, but for some reason gave way to other tall dolls with fantastic bodies. She was also a "Love, American Style" actress: in one episode, her round bed was called the Colosseum, which I thought was wild, like out of *Playboy* or something, but I think it turned out, like it always did on that show, that she wasn't really such a big partyer after all.

Julie costarred with my near-pal Tina in the film *Evils of the Night*. Now she's into real estate and other philosophies.

Quest: Some brassy, self-righteous wise guy with a name that sounds like Zee Ott calls soon after I send the letter and smarmily tells me, on behalf of Ms. Newmar, who has boasted of a 135 IQ, "She was offended by your request, like, *I'm sure*, most women *would* be."

I explain that I have had several positive responses. "Who are these other 'actresses'?" he squawks, as if he either doesn't believe me or else the women who have agreed are just cheap tramps and not committed to their craft. I say that the others have taken it with a sense of humor—setting him back slightly, because nobody wishes to be accused of being humorless—but he recovers.

"*Well*, she was *offended*, and I think she's going to *pass* on this," he whinnies, like a goosed donkey. "I wish you *luck*," he says in closing, as if such clever sarcasm will probably be lost on someone like me. He snaps off the word "pass" with a triumphant nasal inflection, as if I couldn't tell from his initial snotty diatribe where this was going. I wonder, Could this be Rebecca Schaeffer fallout?

K A R E N   V A L É N T I N E

Background: Karen played Alice Johnson, student teacher, on "Room 222." You may remember her from the opening credits: she has trouble with the doors of the bus. She has an appealingly innocent, Gidgety quality that serves her well on a memorable episode of "Love, American Style." (There I go again. Is it just me? I don't think so. "Love, American Style" was, sexually speaking, the most influential TV program in American history. It was ostensibly a chronicle of changing sexual mores, but even us kids knew it was really depicting what a bunch of Hollywood pervos perceived as a Midwesterner's view of the New Morality: it was mild titillation packaged as state-of-the-art orgiastic abandon. But it was better than nothing. Lots better.) In this one, she's a college freshman assigned a male roommate in a coed dorm. Both figure it is just the new, open approach to sexuality, so, although they're uncomfortable, they decide to groove with it. At the end we learn it was all, needless to say, the result of a computer error.

Quest: I send a letter to Karen's agent, Tom Korman. I call a few weeks later to follow up. He "never received it." I send another. I phone. "I sent both letters on to Karen," he says impatiently. "If she wants to do it, you'll hear from her." Both letters? Including the one you never received? What a d*ck.

☞ Post-Mortem:

Barbi probably feels she's been had, but the truth is it looked like about a 50 percent success ratio for a while. All I can say is:

➤ Barbi is *definitely* cool.
➤ Donna and Tina are *sort of* cool.
➤ Lassie, Karen, Elizabeth, Eva, Lee, and Barbara *might* be cool, but should get new agents.
➤ Julie Newmar is definitely *not* cool.

COMPUTATION OF QUEST QUOTIENT

$$QQ = \frac{(M_d/100 + M_f/1000 + P/10 + L/5 + (I \times 10) + D + T) \times DA}{(F/10) + (\$/100) + 1}$$

Mileage driven: $M_d = 4200$
Mileage flown: $M_f = 7000$
Phone calls: $P = 80$
Letters: $L = 18$
Intimacies: $I = 1$
Drop Dead factor: $D = 9$
Days spent: $T = 14$

Difficulty-Aggravation multiplier: $DA = 8$

Failure rate: $F = 90$
Cost: $\$ = 1400$

QUEST QUOTIENT = 31.2

☞ *Analysis:*

This, the questy-est of the quests, posts record highs in several categories. . . . Drop Dead factor figured to be hefty at outset, and didn't disappoint. . . . DA is deceptive: difficulty score is easily a 10-plus, aggravation soars, too, but pleasure of meeting and kissing Barbi and talking to Donna and Tina undermines aggravation—to some extent. . . . Advice to casting agents: it's my observation that Julie Newmar can be "difficult."

THINGS GO BETTER WITH FREE COKE . . .

CASE INSPECTION

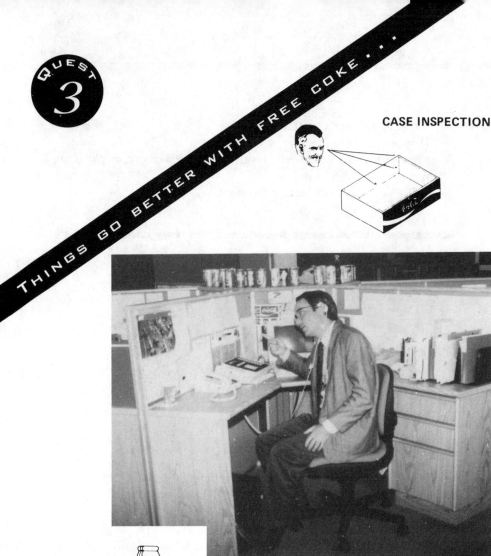

CLEAN
BOTTLE
VISUAL
INSPECTION

The Coca-Cola Hot Line

e've all stared morosely at the dregs of a Fritos bag, tilted it up to our many lips for that last salty spray, and, just before crushing the wrapper in an awesome display of wrist-power, noticed the lines (I

abridge): "Question? Comments? Call 1-800-FLCHIPS." We've for-mulated FLCHIPS questions and comments in our minds, such as, Who would call this number and why? And wouldn't it be fun, I've always thought (no *we* anymore—this is *my* quest), to spend a week manning the 1-800-FLCHIPS hot line, to converse with and inform fellow chipper snackers, to *take an active role in the snack-food econ-omy,* to give something back instead of simply draining its output?

I write to Beverly Holmes, the manager of media relations at Frito-Lay, explaining that "snack food was and is such a great part of my life, and Frito-Lay makes the best snack food (and has the best commercials, too)." (Of course that should read *used to have* the best commercials (I'm talking Frito Bandito, not Jay Leno), but I've worked out this special concept where I try not to be too insulting in my pitches.) My quest, I explain, "is to get involved, deeply involved, and learn more about my favorite snack foods."

What I learn instead is, according to Ms. Holmes, "hot-line staff-ers require six months of training. Besides, there is a lot of *confiden-tial information* involved." Little did I suspect. Apparently I will have to get involved, deeply involved, with a company that harbors no secrets. Says Ms. Holmes, "You might try Coca-Cola. They have a line: 1-800-GET-COKE."

It's true that Coke "adds life," is the "real thing," is "it," and doesn't "rot your teeth": so, I think, why not? Besides, for all the myths about Frito-Lay products—I can't think of any examples right now; there's a rumor that the Diet Coke I pound down affects short-term memory—there are many more about Coca-Cola: What's the deal with Coke and aspirin? Is there less cocaine in Caffeine-Free Coke than in caffeinated Coke? Is New Coke as effective a douche as Classic Coke? If I find a mouse in a bottle, what do I get? Hey, what's in that *secret formula,* anyway? And how come they let a Cuban

(Roberto Goizueta, Chairman of the Board and CEO of the Coca-Cola Company) in on it?

The only downside to Coke is, if Frito-Lay won't let me inside, why should a big giant paranoid megagiant like ultramegagiant Coke? I consider instead attempting to man the lines at the Home Shopping Network, but there's no history, no mystery; many of the calls are broadcast over the air, and nobody ever asks any probing questions. Plus, callers have to give their names, which cuts down on the entertaining cranks that I assume infest such lines as Fritos' and Coke's. The Butterball Turkey hot line looks good, but it only revs up in the fall. Despite the proliferation of consumer hot lines these past few years, there aren't that many that sound really fun.

I send a pitch to Coca-Cola USA, which is based in Atlanta. I soon receive an enthusiastic call from Roger Nunley, the manager of industry and consumer affairs; he is interested in accommodating me and asks for clips of my work. This, to me, is unbelievable. When preparing a quest, you have to ask yourself, What's in it for them? In this case, the Coca-Cola Company has *nothing* to gain, only corporate embarrassment for anybody who approved my quest if it goes haywire. The only way this possibly could have succeeded was through somebody's whim, and apparently Nunley had such a whim. So, despite my not having anything in the old *oeuvre* he will find at all reassuring, I send my clips, and, after a bit of a tussle with the big boys in the adjoining corporate tower, Nunley gives me the thumbs up. Hot-lanta!

I drive down to Georgia with Spunky the Dog for company. When you've got a cute little pup who likes to travel, getting there can be half the fun. Girls at fast-food drive-thru windows melt when he pokes his little black nose out; he's almost always able to cadge a free burger (hold the condiments). Sometimes I even let *him* eat it.

Hurtling down the road with Spunky summons memories of Steinbeck's *Travels with Charley*, a decent book except that Charley was a—ick—French poodle. I might even get ruminative, pontificating for Spunky's benefit, painting a vision of America like Mr. Grapes-O-Wrath himself. Sure, these quests are simply an excuse to get out on the highway, but that doesn't mean there can't be some deeper meaning to it all. How about, for example . . . Native Americans? What's happening with the Proud Red Man?

Like, what do Indians want, and what can we do about it? Spunky and I visit a tiny, neophyte tribe in the middle of North Carolina called the Hattadare. *This* is the way to treat Native Americans, we decide. Hattadare Indian Village, near Bunnlevel, is a homely little theme park fronted by a few old trailers. Spunky romps with a Hattadare chihuahua while I inspect the world's largest Indian arrowhead. After I exchange a few cordial Hows and Ughs with the Hattadare counterman, he informs me that the Hattadares have a dream—they want money from the Great White Father to build a grandiose $5 million pyramid theater in the middle of nowhere in which to present a spectacular play based on the story of the Hattadare. It will be *stupendously spiritual*—the sooner we send them some guilt money the better. Woowoowoowoo!

Travels with Spunky loses its casual, unhurried tone as we are compelled to depart North Carolina by sunset. It seems this is the only state in the USA that forbids cohabitation of humans and canines in motel rooms. My pal Mike, a Durham native, assures me it is the only state that *needs* such a law, if you know what he means.

Bonehead Tarheel State legislators are a distant memory as the Atlanta skyline, including the beloved mirrored-cylinder building from *Sharky's Machine*, bids us an urbane howdy to the New South. I drop off Spunky at his Uncle Dickie's and head off to "work."

Coke's corporate headquarters is a fortresslike compound not far from the Varsity Drive-in, my favorite fast-food establishment excepting the world's largest McDonald's. (At the Varsity, or the Greasy V, as it's known, all customers sit in classroom-style desks pointed at a TV. There are several rooms, each with a TV tuned to a different station. There is no conversation, no human interaction whatsoever once you get your food—it's great!) The Coca-Cola complex comprises two structures: the Coca-Cola USA building and the corporate building, known as the Tower. After driving through the big gates, you pass from one security checkpoint to the next, your name and business being transmitted to the succeeding station before you arrive. I obtain my badge and zoom up to the consumer center.

It's just before 10 A.M.; the phones are not yet humming. I meet my new pal, Roger Nunley, who has arranged a three-day schedule that will take me to each of the various departments there, culminating in my "working the line." It's a respectable agenda, although it falls short of one week. (In fact, I will later discover that on every quest for which I propose to "spend the week," my request is translated as "I'll settle for three days.")

I grill Nunley: "So, what percentage of your calls concern mice in bottles?" Nunley betrays a weary grin as he shakes his head—oh, the misconceptions civilians do have. "Eighty-five percent of the calls are questions about our products," he says, "five percent are suggestions or compliments, and ten percent are complaints: flat product, low fill—no mice in bottles. That just doesn't happen."

We'll see.

The consumer line began in 1983 to get reaction to the new sweetener blend in Tab (which subtly transformed that great metallic bite). The line would soon become the central switchboard of the universe: the Cuban was fixing to tinker with the formula.

The New Coke flurry of 1985 may have sullied Coke's corporate reputation, but it certainly raised the profile of the consumer affairs department. Nunley's eyes mist over as he recalls those turbulent, halcyon days: "The number of employees here went from twenty to one hundred fifty-eight. We went from seven or eight WATS lines to eighty-three. From four hundred calls a day to twelve thousand."

As the historic consumer revolt persisted, a corrective directive came down from the Tower: *Do whatever it takes.* Nunley's budget—previously a matter of typically parsimonious corporate scrutiny—would now be *unlimited.* Middle managers often fantasize of such a catastrophe bringing them to the fore, just as the state trooper daydreams of a speeder's trunk popping open to reveal the French Connection, or the landlady contemplates her fifteen minutes of fame when that weasely new tenant perforates the President.

We all know the rest. New Coke bombed out (just like its spokesdroid, Max Headroom), old Coke was remarketed as Coke Classic, and the overall market share of the two combined—with Classic at Number 1 and New Coke at Number 10—wound up greater than in the first place. Goizueta came out smelling like a fine Havana Dutch Master as the company learned a lesson in brand loyalty the hard but profitable way. The consumer center shrank after the storm blew over; now there are 38 phone agents, called "consumer information specialists," 8 lines, called "lines," and 750 to 1000 calls per day. Maybe the consumer department didn't attain superstardom, but it did establish a solid footing on the ninth floor of the Coca-Cola USA building.

Twelve consumer information specialists are on duty at any one time. They are generally expected to have a college degree in liberal arts, business, or journalism, along with writing skills—each consumer information specialist spends half his hours answering a share of the seventy-five to a hundred letters received per day—and public relations or customer service experience. It's a *team;* they're required to be *enthusiastic.* Why shouldn't they be? They can get wired on free Coke products all day long!

Yes, the best aspect of working here is the Coke machine in the employees' refreshment center. Unlike "street" units that devour coins, this one is free, free, free! Just push a button: whonnnk—a can drops down the chute! Like a wet 'n wild dream!

Between sips, department heads compose guidelines in anticipation of potential queries. The consumer information specialists—let's call them *phone people*—are absolutely forbidden from "winging it." If there is a topic that's not been addressed in their big red book of guidelines, they must tell the caller they will phone him back.

BAD: "So, Mr. Brown, you say you saw an advertisement for Coke on a television program that advocated the wholesale destruction of rain forests in order to build Cuban abortion clinics? Oh, my God! Oh, my God! Would a free lifetime supply of Mr. Pibb be of any comfort, or would you prefer I assist you in organizing a national boycott of our products?"

GOOD: "Thank you for calling today, Mr. Brown; we're very glad to hear you express your feelings on that particular subject today. I'd like to take your phone number and return your call when I can obtain more information on the particular subject that concerns you."

Explosive issues, like South African divestment or the strong possibility that Coke intended to raze Belize rain forests in order to plant Minute Maid orange trees, are first fielded by the media relations department, over in the Tower. There, a positive spin is lovingly applied. In the case of these two issues, Coke was able to wriggle off the hook technically if not morally.

SOUTH AFRICAN DIVESTMENT: "We disinvested in 1986."
   Translation: "We don't support apartheid any more."
BELIZE: "We ended up not planting those orange groves."
   Translation: "Phew—good thing this year's Florida crop came through."

The phone people's manual is packed with mollifying answers to common misconceptions or suspicions about Coke products. Technical questions receive answers read verbatim from the manual; the phone person also follows up these calls by sending a pamphlet that restates what he has said. For example, if a caller is skeptical about Coke's suspiciously vigorous denials about the presence of cocaine in the Formula, he will receive a pamphlet stating, in writing, that there is no cocaine in Coca-Cola.

There is only one subject that is taboo: the contents of the Formula. If you look at the ingredients listed on the can, you will find something called "natural flavors." These are the secret herbs and spices that give Coke its distinctive—yes, distinctive—taste.

First off, I am told, nobody knows the formula except for a few top honchos—including the CEO, who perhaps first tasted *el thingo realisimo* while sucking Cuba Libres from his baby bottle. According to popular legend, the formula is printed on a piece of paper in a vault at the Trust Company Bank in Atlanta; no one I talked to knows the exact setup. Is it in an old, movie-style vault with a big wheel and a time lock? A nondescript safe-deposit box? A box within a safe within a vault? If anybody does know, he'd better not tell me: all employees must sign a pledge not to leak information.

If a caller claims a serious allergy to a particular substance, the phone person might contact the tech department (in the Tower) to verify its nonexistence in Coke—after all, they don't want to kill somebody with a secret ingredient. Of course, this leads to the possibility of somebody—preferably one with a talent for voices—figuring out the formula by trial and error:

RICH LITTLE (as John Wayne): Now listen up, uh, Pilgrim. Is there peanut butter in the formula, or not? I'm allergic.
PHONE PERSON: No, sir, there isn't, and thank you for calling today.
RICH LITTLE (ten minutes later, as Richard Nixon): I would just like to get one thing perfectly clear. Is there cinnamon in the formula? I'm allergic.
PHONE PERSON: Yes, sir, there is, and thank you for calling today.

And so on.

Other touchy subjects include a connection between NutraSweet and short-term memory loss. A doctor at Atlanta's Emory University, which has been heavily endowed by Coke's chairman emeritus Robert Woodruff, claims a causal link, as well as one to behavioral changes. (Like maybe you feel alert and happy?) But NutraSweet tastes good, so inquiries seem to be tailing off.

Calorie levels are not divulged on sugared soft drink cans (it's only required by law on diet sodas), nor is the amount of caffeine listed. A can of Classic Coke has 144 calories (or, as the phone people say, "seventy-two calories per six-ounce serving"), while New Coke has 154. (Could *calories* be one of the New ingredients?) Both contain 46 milligrams of caffeine, or, as the phone people explain, "about one-fourth the amount of caffeine in the same quantity of brewed coffee." Not that there's anything wrong with caffeine; a brochure is sent to the caller explaining that "throughout history, people of the world have chosen caffeine-containing beverages for refreshment and as a basis for social interaction" and "caffeine forms part of a beverage flavor profile in whatever soft drink it is used" (and is not there just to give you a buzz or anything). What are they so defensive about? *Caffeine is great!*

Occasionally a globe-trotting Cokehead will wonder why ingredients are not listed on the container in some countries. "It is our observation," says the manual and thus the phone person, "that consumers in various countries do not have the same level of interest regarding ingredients present in food products."

EXT: FOREIGN CAFE: NIGHT

FOREIGN WOMAN
(holding up bottle of bright blue liquid)
Zoot allures! What eez zees food product?

FOREIGN MAN
(grabbing bottle, drinks contents lustily)
Oo cares? Le glug-glug-glug.

FOREIGN WOMAN
(raising bottle of Liquid Drano to lips)
Oui, oui—oo cares!

A final, crucial bit of information concerns the bottling process. The Coca-Cola Company produces, at several locations, the syrup concentrate that will become Coke, but the actual bottling is done by local bottlers, of which there are 418 (as of this writing; the number has been decreasing steadily—ten years ago there were 550) in the

U.S. Thus, any complaint related to the product—flatness, half-filled can, nonavailability, botched packaging, mouse—is a darn shame indeed, and we're very sorry, but it is not the fault of the company; it is the responsibility of a local bottler.

My first huddle is with Lynn Henkel, who oversees consumer correspondence. Product complaints, called "quality control questions," are passed on to local bottlers, who might do nothing, might send a letter of apology, might even show up at the consumer's front door bearing a six-pack, which would be truly neat, don't you think?

The variety of other "questions" concern just about any topic that is currently in the news: Coke has become interwoven, so to speak, with the fabric of the American flag. When the *Exxon Valdez* drunkenly dumped oil into Prince William Sound, consumers started beefing to Coke about it. Why Coke? Because, incredibly, customers spotted *Coke machines* at Exxon gas stations, like it would be okay to sell Coke at Mobil or Texaco stations, for example, but not at Exxon because Exxon is a huge faceless corporation that thinks the environment is simply someplace to foul up or drill in, while all the other big gas companies are like Floyd's Oil, your good pals down the block, and they would send their CEO personally to wipe the sludge off each and every little birdy that got soiled in the unlikely event that *they* would ever experience such a disaster.

One lady wrote to Coca-Cola wanting five dollars; she said she was writing different companies asking for five dollars. No luck here, but sounds like one-tenth of a great book idea. Lynn, like many here a true Coke aficionada, shows me some Coke oddities she has gleaned in her travels, such as an experimental clear-plastic Sprite can and a canned coffee beverage called Georgia Coffee ("It's pretty good," she says. "Very popular in Japan.")

Okay, but what about the nutballs? The Coca-Cola Company won't respond to totally incomprehensible letters, she admits, but these represent a very small portion of all correspondence. "We used to keep a 'funny file,' but we moved our files and cleaned a lot of stuff out," she says, sorry to see my disappointment.

People seem to write for one of two reasons: 1) they think Coke will be so remorseful for their incredibly minor inconvenience that they will be awarded a lifetime supply; or, 2) they are insufferably neurotic and know that a company with a reputation for consumer responsiveness like Coke will take them seriously.

I next meet with Donna Bracewell, who is responsible for relaying product and packaging complaints to local bottlers. One advantage to this centralized system for consumer response is that the company can watch for patterns, such as Diet Coke that repeatedly tastes like root beer. She will send a letter to every complainant, but there is no set policy about providing refunds or coupons—it can depend on the tone of the complaint. (Besides, it's up to the local bottler to make it right with the consumer.)

The department does a quarterly survey of past consumer calls as a follow-up; they survey bottlers as well. Like the company, Donna tells me, the bottlers are becoming more consumer-oriented. It's a lot of trouble over a twelve-ounce soft drink, but this is what makes Coca-Cola what it is, and it's hard to argue with that. Common complaints are hardly earthshaking: empty can, wrong product in can, suspicion that Classic is not old Coke, soda that tastes like it's exceeded its shelf life (which for sugared drinks is nine to eighteen months; diet drinks, three to six months).

"How about mice in bottles?" I ask, impishly reiterating a theme that will have them comparing notes and shaking their heads after I leave. "There have been no mouse-in-bottle complaints," she replies. I kick myself later: *I never asked about mice in cans!*

I wonder about restaurants where they serve only Pepsi (known here as The "P" Word): at these places, I like to ask for Coke anyway just to see what they'll say. They almost never say, to quote dead fat *Wired* character John Belushi, "No Coke—Pepsi." Donna tells me the Trade Research department will go into a restaurant and ensure "Coke" is genuine Coca-Cola, or that if you order Coke and they have another brand they will inform you. This, I think, would be one of the best jobs in the world, although my pal Mike still thinks being the head of the Bureau of Alcohol, Tobacco, and Firearms would be the best, and I can see his point.

I meet with Ann Francis, who is not the sultry star of "Honey West," that great '60s female-detective show, but is an earnest woman who negotiates the minefields of idea submissions and ingredient inquiries.

Coca-Cola cannot accept idea submissions regarding advertising, sales promotions, modifications of existing products or concepts that have already been considered and discarded in-house, this last one being the hardest to prove or disprove. My assumption is that no company this size has any interest in outside ideas—this can only lead to trouble. But, I am assured, if an idea fits the guidelines, it will be presented to the appropriate department.

An idea for a piece of equipment is the likeliest to get anywhere. Ms. Francis tells me, to my surprise, that they've had no major problems with infringement on outside ideas. About one in twenty-five letters goes on to the next step; there are three thousand to four thousand submissions each year.

No wacky ideas come to mind, Ms. Francis tells me—but wait: "There was one man who proposed a three-liter bottle with one-third Coke, one-third Diet Coke, and one-third Cherry Coke. He even supplied a diagram."

Too-oo-oot! Yubba dubba do, it's lunchtime, and the employee cafeteria is a cheery place indeed. A cornucopia awaits; meals are subsidized, and Coca-Cola Company soft drinks flow like the Chattahoochie. Food is paid for with magnetized I.D. cards—if this is *1984*, I can't wait! If only this place had TV, it would be even better than the Varsity. Ha ha—too bad *you'll* never get to eat here!

After lunch, I get to monitor the phone lines and observe Claire Jackson, a senior associate in consumer correspondence, as she supervises the other phone people. Right off the bat, a woman calls to say she is offended by a Coke TV commercial that features Madeline Kahn and a hokey, cartoony ghost. She (the moron lady, not Ms. Kahn) is convinced that this glorifies Satan. (I assume she is referring to the ghost; I mean, if overrated comediennes were satanic, wouldn't Whoopi Goldberg be able to levitate stadiums and stuff?) I would have replied, "Yeah, so?," but cooler heads prevail and the woman is pacified.

The phone people have attracted an amusing cast of regular callers, sort of like Bob's patients on the old "Newhart." One guy who had originally wanted to submit an idea for a mint soda now calls to "rap." "People from Alaska call during the winter just to talk," says Claire.

"People will ask where we are, and when they find out Atlanta, they'll say, 'I thought so by your accent,' or they'll ask, 'How's the weather?' " she says, smiling and crinkling her nose at the common humanity thing of it all. I'm not saying these callers are banal or anything, but just remember if you call the hot line and say these things you are not exactly being original.

There is one highlight: a call from Wisconsin about an exploding bottle. "The rescue squad had to come and treat me," the caller says, as if he is proud of this. The correct response: "And was this bottle stored at room temperature?"

I spend some time perusing the manual and learn many fascinating tidbits about Coke products. For instance: How was Tab named? "We programmed a computer to print every three- and four-letter word in the English language which contained either a vowel or a consonant [?]. This is in line with research which tells us short trademarks are remembered more easily by the public than long ones. Out of approximately 250,000 words, the list was narrowed, the validity of the trademarks checked out, and from that list, Tab was selected."

Two cookbooks are made available by the consumer center: *Cooking with Coca-Cola* and *International Cooking with Coca-Cola*, both chock-full of recipes for delicious dishes made even more taste-tempting by the presence of our favorite soft drink. (Call and they'll send you a copy.) I am also apprised of the awesome gamut of Coke products that may not be apparent to you if your local bottler neglects to supply such flavors as Fanta Bubble Gum or Banana sodas.

Say, what *are* those intermittent rumblings? Oh. It seems the free Coke that the phone people have been knocking back all day long has yielded a roomful of demure Southern belles quietly suppressing belches.

Before I am ready to solo, I get some more background from Amy Treend, the project manager for consumer education. New employees, I am told, receive a week of training: listening to calls, using a computer as if answering a real call, being monitored from another room. I am on an accelerated schedule, known as the Three Day Week. All calls to the center are taped and logged on computer. Monday is the heaviest day: people drink Coke on the weekend, see the 800 number, and get curious.

I am handed a form that phone people are supposed to fill out in the event of receiving a product-tampering threat over the 800 line. Phone people are told to ask the (presumably dumb as a thumb) terrorist a list of questions that includes "Where is the contaminated product right now?"; "What is your name?"; and "What is your address?"

Time to hit the phones! I get a cranky oldster venting his anger about the new bottom on the two-liter bottle: it won't stand up in his fridge. "It keeps tipping over—CLUNK. Spills over everything. You should provide flat trays for us to put the bottles on." He's right; the bottoms were probably changed for reasons of production economy, and they don't stand up too well on wire refrigerator shelves. "That's a great idea. Maybe you should take a tray and try that," I suggest. "Yeah, maybe I'll try that," he says, clearly hoping for more action but cynically figuring I'm going to hang up and forget all about him. I take his name and address; because he claimed to be such a longtime loyal Coke drinker and felt that the company didn't care about his problem, we will send him a letter acknowledging his call and letting him know we passed his complaint on to the packaging department.

Most calls are boring. More complaints about the new two-liter bottom: one woman moans that it knocked over her Jell-O. All the while, Amy sits next to me and monitors. I am doing okay. A call comes in with a product complaint that I am not equipped to answer. I put it on hold. "Don't say you'll put her on with your supervisor," Amy says. "She'll think it's some kind of big deal then."

"I'll put you on with the person who handles that specific area of inquiry," I tell the woman. This is a pretty decent way of handling it. Even so, I am once again performing a quest in which I set out to "work" but end up mostly observing. People ask me of these quests, "Did they pay you?" Of course I am never paid; I never do anything. Besides, pay at the sort of jobs at which I've been questing is pretty negligible.

My final day I am paired, appropriately, with young Rebecca Smith; it's her last day, too. She's going to work at the Trust Company Bank, where the Formula is stored. The calls are about the same as before; there are more complaints than the 10 percent Nunley described, but most callers are, like me, pretty big fans of the product and simply curious about the 800 number.

My pal Mike had promised to call today with the following:

"I put my son's baby tooth in a glass of Coke, and the next morning it was all dissolved."

The phone person will then jump in and explain that this is not a valid experiment, because the chemical makeup of the human mouth prevents this sort of decay.

But Mike will interrupt: "What I want to know is, is it okay to drink that glass of Coke now?"

The idea is, the phone person will rush to tell me about the weird call she just got, and I will be able to report this as a real call. A pseudoevent, just like the big boys do!

Unfortunately, Mike is busy merging banks and forgets.

A pleasant woman calls from Farragut, Iowa. She begins almost apologetically, but then the words gush out in a fizzy torrent. "I poured out the contents of the can into a glass, and there were what looked like . . . *bones* inside. I took it back to the grocery store, and the manager inspected it, and he was sure it was a dead mouse."

A mouse in a can! Rebecca is silent, looking at me like, "This guy is never going to believe this doesn't ever happen." The woman is very sweet, and she explains, "I wanted you to know about it."

Will this woman be getting a whole swimming pool of free Coke? Maybe. Should I include this in my story? It does give a funny, ironic twist to conclude the quest. But the fact is, no matter how pro-Coca-Cola I've been to this point, the only thing people—especially my pals at the consumer info center—will remember about what I've written is the woman who said she found a mouse in a can.

What I need is a flashback to all the positive verbiage of yesteryear. Remember how responsive the company is to consumer input, how committed Coca-Cola has always been to quality? Good, because I have a duty to report the truth. Especially when it's funny and ironic.

☆ ☆ ☆ ☆ ☆ ☆ ☆ ☆ ☆ ☆ ☆ ☆ ☆ ☆ ☆ ☆ ☆ ☆

When in Rome...

HI, REV. FIN$TER!

A very artful way to kill an Atlanta afternoon (besides attending a taping of the CNN evening news) is to drive an hour and a half northwest to Summerville, which is near Rome, which is famous for having been built, unlike its fetid Italian counterpart, in a day. (Or maybe it was *destroyed* in a day. I'm not sure; you can't tell by looking at it.) Summerville is home to the Reverend Howard Finster, who has been anointed the folk artist of choice by the "hep" rock & roll crowd, especially David Byrne and the moody wimps of REM. My pal Mike and I visited Finster, who is seventysomething, several years ago while researching a vitally important story on rock tourism. He preached our ears off for hours—"Jesus said this, blah blah blah, Ezekias said that"—but we had fun (he also told us that the previous night he had met Adolf Hitler in a dream. The nasty Nazi was looking down at his feet, being so embarrassed for what he'd done; Finster turned to him and said, "Man, you are a *fool*"), and Mike bought some art: Finster's famous *Elvis at 3* cutout and a dinosaur with hand-lettered gospelish quotes condemning cocaine.

I drive up the morning after my last day at Coke, dreading another blazing preachment but wanting to score some art as a wedding gift. I arrive around ten-thirty; the Rev is still aslumber. His wife says he was up till *two in the morning*, working. I wait, and let Spunky loose to romp with the local dog pack.

Finster arises, hacks out the accumulated old-man mucus of the night, and invites me into his salon, telling me, stolid and ninja-like, that he was toiling until, oh, *four in the morning*. He says he is over-worked but must fulfill his mission, which is the mass production of cookie-cutter folk art for tourists. Unlike my last visit, when the Rev admitted Mike and me to his actual studio and displayed his still-wet creations only after discerning our intentions and degree of godliness, this time I find myself in the showroom of the proverbial "cottage-cheese industry." The Reverend now displays a varied inventory of art commodities, each priced with a tag. He's had printed a line of posters, and the verbose preachments on his three-dimensional fig-ures, formerly handwritten, are now pasted-on Xeroxes.

With nary a "Jesus," he pitches his colorful rendition of a Coca-Cola bottle, which seems an appropriate purchase indeed, even at two hundred fifty bucks. (Finster, too, has had a lifelong affection for Coke.) "You won't lose money on this," he says, used-car-dealer-like. "I get eighteen hundred for 'em in galleries."

"But I don't want to resell it, I want to put it on my wall," I explain —not that I am haggling.

"Well, they cost two fifty and they're worth eighteen hundred."

I load the trunk with a Coke bottle, a couple of Elvises, and an Abraham Lincoln. (Finster uses the obverse of a Lincoln penny as his model.) Spunky has loaded up on souvenirs, too—a lively tribe of Georgia fleas.

COMPUTATION OF QUEST QUOTIENT

$$QQ = \frac{(M_d/100 + M_f/1000 + P/10 + L/5 + (I \times 10) + D + T) \times DA}{(F/10) + (\$/100) + 1}$$

Mileage driven: $M_d = 1950$
Mileage flown: $M_f = 0$
Phone calls: $P = 6$
Letters: $L = 3$
Intimacies: $I = 0$
Drop Dead factor: $D = 1$
Days spent: $T = 6$

Difficulty-Aggravation multiplier: $DA = 5$

Failure rate: $F = 0$
Cost: $\$ = 600$

QUEST QUOTIENT = 19.8

☞ *A n a l y s i s :*

A robust quest indeed! . . . An arithmetic-alish roller coaster of highs and lows: high Anticipated Difficulty number counterbalanced by low Aggregate Aggravation . . . many miles traveled offset by costliness of journey. . . . The D, or so-called Drop Dead factor, could have included entire North Carolina state legislature, but, since quest occurred in Georgia, conscience vetoed.

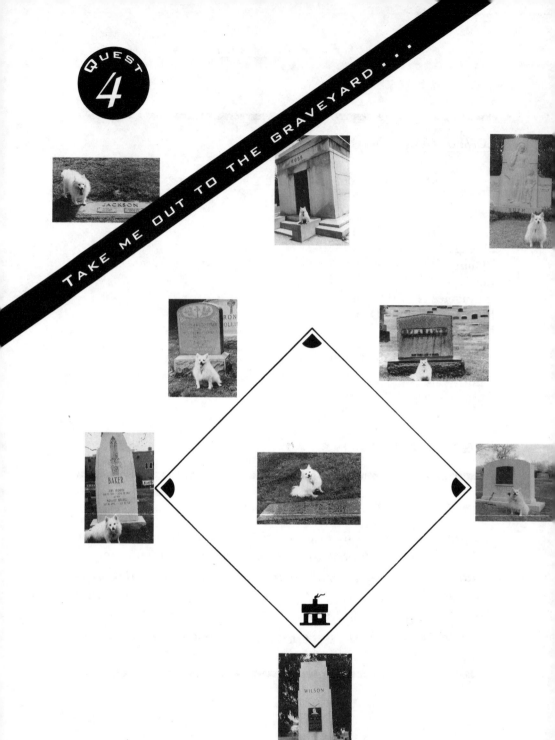

TAKE ME OUT TO THE GRAVEYARD . . .

Spunky's Dream Team

★ ★ ★ ute puppies and ★ ★
★ ★ eternal glory. Add ★ ★
★ a splash of sex and you've got ★
★ the essence of the American ★
★ dream. Forget the sex—espe- ★
★ cially if you're in North Caro- ★
★ lina—and you've got the next ★
★ quest. . . . ★

These days, the only time you can get within one hundred feet of a baseball idol is for the 1.7 seconds it takes for him to sign a fifteen-dollar autograph. Why bother? The idea is to bask in a hero's greatness, not to behold his blotchy skin and bleary eyes. There *is*, however, a subterranean sect of diamond legends who'll let you linger as long as you like, who'll pose for photos without objection, who were genuinely worthier than today's nicknameless millionaire stiffs on expansion-diluted rosters who call themselves superstars but can't even bunt. That's right: today's fan has one last refuge—the cemetery.

More and more, I find cemeteries the only roadside attractions that maintain that classic feeling. Think about it:

➤ Always plenty of free parking.
➤ Natural grass, no domes.
➤ You can "bring your own (BYO)."
➤ Unlike the majority of truly idiosyncratic, noteworthy structures, mausoleums don't get new signs and mansard roofs every few years.
➤ You'll hardly ever end up driving five hours only to find that the cemetery went out of business six months ago.
➤ The grounds are real bucolic and nobody bothers you unless you start spray-painting swastikas.
➤ All legends die. And now they're out there, unshielded by bodyguards, gates, and alarms; all there is between you and them is six feet of dirt!

My initial idea is to track down the greatest starting lineup of all time, which is generally conceded to be that of the 1927 New York Yankees, known as Murderers Row. The first snag is that Mark Koenig, the team's shortstop, is still alive. The next is that the Yankee flacks are lazy and uncooperative, the graves difficult to locate. Finally, I remember something: I *hate* the "God Damn Yankees." So the hell with 'em.

Better yet, I will create an all-time dream team. To qualify, players had to have a movie made about them, a cool nickname, or something peculiar about their life or death. And, certainly, they had to be dead: the one-armed wartime outfielder Pete Gray (played by Keith "I'm Easy" Carradine in a TV movie) was a top contender for the squad until I discovered he is alive and living in Pennsylvania. Likewise drawing breath, unfortunately, is Steve "On a Scale of One to Ten, If Ted Bundy's a Ten, Then He's a Seven" Garvey, whose lucky banjo homer in the fourth game of the 1984 playoffs denied the Cubbies a World Series. Only our third runner-up, William Hoy—who was nicknamed "Dummy" because he was a deaf mute—managed to die.

Baseball is something that should be shared by father and son, owner and dog. So my canine, Spunky, and I hit the road in search of excellence (or, as they say in Indiana, *exellence)*, and here, ladies and gentlemen, boys and girls, is the starting lineup. Get your pencils and score cards ready.

Graveyard fever—catch it!

THE LINEUP

Leading off, the Centerfielder:
TYRUS RAYMOND "TY" COBB, Village Cemetery, Royston, Georgia

As you cross the boundary line of a sleepy little town in northeast Georgia, you encounter a well-maintained, classically styled billboard

TY COBB

—an action pose. A man in an old Detroit Tigers uniform is rounding a base, slyly making a dash for the next. WELCOME TO ROYSTON, reads the sign, HOME OF BASEBALL'S IMMORTAL TY COBB. Soon you cross Ty Cobb Street. Down the road is the Ty Cobb Civic Center, which exhibits a noble statue and plaque out front. Royston may be one of those stagnant Southern towns that focuses hopelessly on bygone days, endlessly trumpeting its heritage, but in this case it's excusable: at least you don't have to learn about yet another boring Civil War skirmish or visit a plantation mysteriously devoid of slave quarters. In fact, given the paucity of unreservedly *proud* ballplayer hometowns across the land, Royston is a downright de-lite.

Ty Cobb's scrappy offensive prowess on the baseball diamond is indisputable, the stuff of legend. His offensiveness off the field—which included not only unsavory deportment but also gambling and throwing ballgames—has been duly noted as well.

So what? An inventory of exalted men and women who were also impeccable of character can be tallied on the fingers of Mordecai Brown's right hand; egocentric, conscience-free superachievers are as abundant as the hairs on Steve Garvey's gorilla forearms. History, sanitized for your convenience, forgives the talented sinner—or, better still, forgets his sins: those whose "off-field" trespasses have *not* been glossed over are simply unlucky. Besides, Cobb's greatness can be measured statistically, while his vileness can never be quantified: Most second basemen spiked in a season? Highest career percentage of little kids snubbed? No way. Forget it.

Even if Cobb had not fashioned such a glorious playing career, he would still be remembered around these parts for another accomplishment that brought him acclaim and envy: he died a very wealthy man, having invested wisely in Coca-Cola. (He was an occasional hunting pal of Coke boss Robert Woodruff and received such inside tips as, "We got George Michael on board, Ty. And Whitney Houston. Go for it!") Cobb's magnificent mausoleum dwarfs the tiny dogs that come by to pay him tribute. The Georgia Peach (nice appropriate nickname—*not!*) will forever—at least until we are invaded by Japan and players get inducted into the Hall of Fame on the basis of how nice they were to their grandparents—be a force to be reckoned with.

Batting 2nd, the Leftfielder:
JOSEPH JEFFERSON "SHOELESS JOE" JACKSON, Woodlawn
Memorial Park, Greenville, South Carolina

SPUNKY'S DREAM TEAM

JOE JACKSON

If Joe Jackson were ever going to be redeemed, to be evaluated, like other players, on his statistics and on-field accomplishments instead of on the fascist pronouncement of a few self-absorbed rich monopolists, this would be the time. Two recent movies—*Eight Men Out* and *Field of Dreams*—proclaim Joe's innocence; the average fan of today, having no firsthand recollection of Joe's play or his involvement in the Black Sox scandal, certainly should have no objection to his being inducted into the Hall of Fame. But the average fan has no say in the matter: only the Hall of Fame's doddering veterans committee is in a position to install Joe Jackson, who has the third highest lifetime batting average in history, in his rightful place in the sports pantheon.

No, unless you're on that damn veterans committee, there's not much you can do except call radio phone-in shows and make an ass of yourself. The only chance the little guy has to express himself is on the All-Star ballot, and even *that* might get taken away. But until it does . . . why not pen in a write-in vote for Joe Jackson in the American League outfield? Okay, so they *won't* let him play—but talk about sending a message!

With Shoeless Joe's national reputation on the rise, surely his hometown of Greenville, South Carolina, must be embracing him to its municipal bosom. I wanted Spunky to see what civic outpouring was *really* all about; after all, Royston may have done right by Cobb, but Royston is a town of modest means, and it's likely local enthusiasm was dampened by Cobb's nasty disposition. Jackson, on the other hand, was by all accounts a gentle, quiet man who prospered as a merchant after his "retirement," and his beloved Greenville has grown into a substantial metropolis. (Bob Jones University, the only college that sounds like it was named after a baseball player, is located here.)

We pass the city limits sign: no mention of Greenville's most famous son. Joe is buried at a memorial park, so there aren't any elaborate tombstones; his gravesite is marked by a simple ground plaque. Spunky is a tad agitated as we prepare to get out of the car and pay our respects; I think that pig-out at the Beacon Drive-In in Spartanburg might be disagreeing with him.

Yes indeed. Spunky, proclaiming an excretory fascination with the graves of ballplayers, lets it all out on poor Joe. I am disappointed; no dog of mine should poop on a man when he's down. But he does, for protracted minutes—a dark comedy of excess. The dog's sense of irony is as pungent as the atmosphere in our motel room that night.

The next day we visit Lester Erwin, a local high school baseball coach who is working to clear Jackson's name. (Mrs. Shoeless Joe and Erwin's mother were cousins.) Erwin has assembled a smattering of memorabilia he will contribute to a Joe Jackson museum if one ever materializes: one of Joe's bats (not the fabled Black Betsy), his driver's license, letters, a cable from a "mole" inside Comiskey's lawyer's office advising Joe to get a good attorney because the sleazy Old Roman is out for blood, and a ball. There are no gloves or shoes: after all these years of Joe's being criminally undervalued, it seems likely a lot of his mementos have been lost forever.

According to Eliot Asinof's *Eight Men Out*, Joe received and kept five thousand dollars before the 1919 World Series, and his productivity *was* affected; it's implied that on some plays Joe tried harder than on others, and that he became upset and confused as to what he should do. Walter Gropman's *Say It Ain't So, Joe* falls back on Joe's outstanding series stats as evidence that he gave 100 percent. Either way, there's no way of proving whether he did or didn't try to throw the series. All we know is he took the money.

Erwin is distressed at the lack of local support: he campaigned for a statue outside the town's ballpark (Greenville has a Class AA Braves team) and a WELCOME TO GREENVILLE, HOME OF SHOELESS JOE JACKSON sign, but even in Joe's hometown, old injustices run deep. Bill Workman, the mayor of Greenville, wouldn't even sanction the no-cost option of naming the ballpark after Joe: he didn't want to offend residents who idiotically wanted it named after *their* Mill League ancestors—none of whom ever made the pros, let alone hit a career .356. Do you think anyone in Royston had the nerve to equate *his* ancestor's baseball skills with those of *Cobb?*

There is one potential source of funds for a statue, however: John Sayles, who directed *Eight Men Out* and publicly bemoans Joe's raw deal—"waaah, waaah, capitalist oppression, boo-hoo-hoo"—received a MacArthur Foundation "genius" grant, money that is supposed to free the recipient from earthly constraints so he may do sublime genius things, like writing anemic Hollywood screenplays. If Sayles would contribute his genius money, Shoeless Joe could be on the road to Cooperstown. I'll toss in 10 percent of my royalties from this book. So c'mon, John Sayles: put your genius money where your mouth is.

Batting 3rd, the Rightfielder:
GEORGE HERMAN "BABE" RUTH, Gate of Heaven Cemetery,
Hawthorne, New York
and . . .

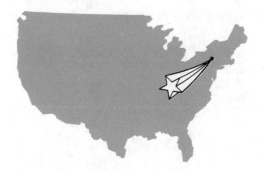

Batting cleanup, playing First Base:
HENRY LOUIS "LOU" GEHRIG, Kensico Cemetery, Valhalla, New
York

SPUNKY'S DREAM TEAM

LOU GEHRIG

And now, a flashback . . .

It was Lou and the Bambino who first got Spunky involved in this
quest. The Spunker and I visited Babe Ruth first; the Bambino rests
just a few miles up the road from the Iron Horse. Babe's impressive
interment has brought many a man to tears; with Spunky, the fluids
flowed from another duct. This, I thought at the time, was not particularly notable, since Spunky had been cooped up in the car for ninety
minutes. As I had not been watching for this behavior, I failed to
capture the moment on film.

Thirty minutes later, I'm searching for the grave of the "Luckiest

Man on the Face of the Earth." Spunky hops out when I park and makes a beeline for, oddly enough, Gehrig's grave. This time, I dash over with my camera in hopes of "freezing the action"; however, I am too late—the amber deed is done. Nonetheless, it makes me wonder whether Spunky holds some ancestral grudge against these great sluggers of the 1920s and '30s. Was the little spitz, in a former life:

➤ Wally Pipp, the Yankee first baseman for whom, one day in 1925, Gehrig permanently substituted?
➤ Guy Bush, the pitcher who became an athlete's-footnote to history when he served up Babe's 714th (and final) home run in 1935?
➤ A disgruntled Boston Red Sox fan, still unforgiving over the trade that sent Ruth to the despised New York Yankees in exchange for $125,000 cash plus a loan?
➤ An A.L.S. victim who wanted the disease to be named after *him?*
➤ A husband whom Babe cuckolded?

Or did the poor, deluded pooch just think he was peeing on Steve Garvey?

Spunky's strange behavior made me want to investigate the other all-time greats, and the result is this quest.

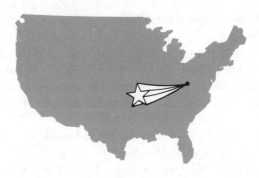

Batting 5th, the Catcher:
LEWIS ROBERT "HACK" WILSON, Rosedale Cemetery, Martinsburg, West Virginia

HACK WILSON

Poor Hack Wilson. In 1930 he hit 56 homers, a National League record, and drove in 190 runs, a major-league record. Yet it wasn't until 1979 that he was finally admitted to Cooperstown. His twelve-year career was brief by Hall of Fame standards, his best season is denigrated as a *"sniff*—hitter's year," and he did not have a great reputation, humanity-wise; but such hypocritical nitpicking does not deter Spunky and me from proudly playing this prodigious Cub catcher on our heavenly (or whatever) nine. (Okay—he was an outfielder. By the time he reached the Cubs, 1926, Gabby Hartnett—whose bowling alley was *the* hangout in Lincolnwood, Illinois, where I grew up—was entrenched at the position, and Hack already pigeonholed as a centerfielder. But Hack would have been a great catcher; he had the nickname and build—5–6, 190 pounds—for it. At last he gets his chance to don the proverbial "tools of idiocy.")

Martinsburg, West Virginia, is not the town to which John Denver wants his beloved country roads, Mountain Mama, to take him home. In fact, this ramshackle community is the kind that expectantly hopes to attract a religious cult or radioactive-waste dump. No offense, but the gas-station guy has given us bogus directions, and we're seeing more than the optimum amount of Martinsburg. Stray dogs, coupling at will on main thoroughfares, send Spunky into a yelping frenzy; the proud hound has forgotten his mission.

I finally find the graveyard, thanks to the patient help of a man at a Quik Stop. I don't get his name, because I'm not the kind of guy who asks people's names. This may be journalistically irresponsible, but think how a normal person reacts when you ask his name for no apparent reason. He assumes:

➤ You want to have homosexual relations with him.
➤ You are going to rob his house.
➤ You are serving a summons, then want to have homosexual relations with him, rob his house, steal his car, and sue him.

If you need a name for the man at the Quik Stop—if you think this is fiction, where the author can give a name to anybody he wants —it is Frank Peterson. From now on, all the people I deal with whose names don't really matter are Frank Peterson.

Hack's grave is impressive: a ten-foot-high granite block. A local booster commissioned a bronze plaque with a Hall of Fame–ish look; it is attached to the face of the tombstone beneath a pair of crossed bats. "We don't get many visitors to that grave," a cemetery exec, Frank Peterson, tells me. "Maybe a few a year."

"Hack," thinks Spunky, "we hardly knew ye."

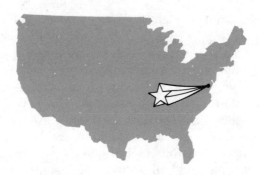

Batting 6th, the Third Baseman:
JOHN FRANKLIN "HOME RUN" BAKER, Spring Hill Cemetery,
Easton, Maryland

Traveling with a dog, the proverbial "man's only friend," has its
downside:

➤ When you leave him alone in the car in 90-degree heat you have to remember to crack the window open a bit.

➤ When he throws up in the car you can't just go and sit in the other room.

➤ North Carolina.

But with Spunky, the real trouble began when he learned how—and when—to honk the horn. I was at an outdoor pay phone near Pocomoke City, Maryland, standing right outside the car; Spunky was waiting in the driver's seat. The pooch impatiently shifted his weight onto the steering wheel, causing the horn to sound. The blaring was hard to ignore; Spunky refused to budge as I banged on the window, so I abridged my call. I ordered Spunky off the horn and got back inside. All *he* knew was:

➤ I leaned on the steering wheel
➤ It made a big noise
➤ And Daddy came back.

This sequence of events was not lost on him. I may be the only one who can open a can of Grand Gourmet, but now he has some leverage, too.

We chose Home Run Baker because we figured that even by wimpy, pre–Babe Ruth standards, this guy's home-run totals were so paltry that this had to be an early example of nickname sarcasm, like calling a bald guy "Curly" or a total sleaze "Madonna," and we felt sorry for him. We pulled into the graveyard at closing time: the groundskeeper, Frank Peterson, let us in, asking if we could latch the gate on our way out. I set Spunky loose, commanding him to find the gravesite quickly, as our light was fading. Spunky, preoccupied with hatching new schemes to bedevil Dad, was unable to sniff out the Duke of Dink. Finding graves in these medium-sized cemeteries can be a mission impossible. The larger facilities distribute maps and celebrity lists, but at these darn medium-sized cems you've really got to comb the grounds.

Finally, we locate the white stone. Baker's heirs saw to it that his avocation would always be remembered: a bat, a glove, and a ball are chiseled onto the marker, along with some holy leafs and stuff. His eternal soul may be off on a "road trip," it says, but his corporeal self reposes in one posh clubhouse.

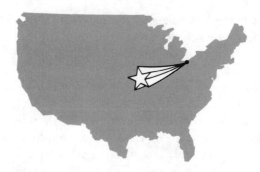

Batting 7th, the Second Baseman:
EDWARD JAMES "BIG ED" DELAHANTY, Calvary Cemetery,
Cleveland, Ohio

BIG ED DELAHANTY

Big Ed's mysterious, dramatic death overshadowed an illustrious career and unmatched fivefold sibling rivalry—brothers Frank, Jim, Joe, and Tom all played in the bigs—that eclipsed even that of Felipe Alou and his brothers, Jesus, Mary, and Joe. The fatal scenario, related to us by Joe Overfield, a Buffalo baseball historian, is that on the night of July 2, 1903, Delahanty was ejected from a train in Bridgeburg, Ontario, for being drunk and disorderly. Staggering away, he fell off a railroad bridge and plummeted into the Niagara River. A week later, the carcass of the Hall of Fame sometime second baseman was found twenty miles downriver, at the foot of the Horseshoe Falls.

. . .

Spunky and I spend an entire Friday barreling cross-country from western Indiana, hydroplaning under a veritable Niagara of thunder-showers, in an attempt to reach Big Ed's Cleveland gravesite before the cemetery office closes. If we take no food breaks and make but the briefest of pit stops, see no sights, drive about 20 m.p.h. too fast for conditions, and don't die, we will reach the gates at about 4 P.M.

We would have made it, too, if not for pokey Buckeye Staters and a construction snarl along I-77. By three-thirty that afternoon, we have finally outdriven the storm, but are still over an hour from Cal-vary Cemetery. I pull over at a rest stop to phone the graveyard. If someone will tell me the location of Big Ed, we can pull in around 5 P.M.—the office will be closed, but the grounds are open till dusk—and snap the photo, continue driving east, and put a good eight to twelve hours between us and the rain.

I have placed too much faith in the chipper helpfulness of ceme-tery employees, especially on a TGIF afternoon. The man who an-swers the phone, Frank Peterson, is aghast at my request:

"Do you know how *large* Calvary Cemetery is?"

"Now I do," I reply. "Aren't the sections numbered?"

HOOOOOOOOONK! Spunky is anxious to get back on the road.

"You'll never find it. This office closes at four-thirty. There are tens of thousands of graves here," he says, boasting.

"Will you tell me the section number and let me take my chances?"

HOOOOOOOONK!

"You just come in tomorrow and we'll give you the information then."

"But I want to reach Olean, New York, tonight. There's a big storm headed this way; I spent the whole day driving through it and don't want to have to do it all over again," I say, although at this point the idea of playing to his "sympathy" is ludicrous. "Can you leave a map with the guard?"

"With the *guard?!* Look, come into the office tomorrow. We open at eight-thirty."

I am stranded in Cleveland with a killer storm front on the way; another day of miserable driving looms. My easygoing self taxed past endurance, I decide to embark on a miniquest: a search for a nice, cheap motel that allows pets and has WTBS in the rooms. (The sixth game of the Bulls-Knicks playoffs is on that night.)

The first few places I try scoff at my requirements. "You'll never find all those things," they taunt. "Ohhh, what a cute dog."

"We'll see, cackle-cackle-cackle," I say.

Eventually, I do find the perfect place. Steely resolve *can* be rewarded, I discover—still, the thrill of accomplishment does not offset the frustration of failing when you're *really* trying. An armor of apathy is the only defense against outright implosion, where you get so mad your head bursts. Right, Spunky?

Arrrrr . . . ruuuuuuff! (Sounds like "R-u-u-uth!")

No, you kooky canine—*Delahanty!*

The next morning, rain pummels the car like bottomless pitchers of Canadian beer as we creep toward our rendezvous with Big Ed. We get his location and a map at the office, then ride, not needing the map at all, to the well-marked section; the Delahanty stone is visible from the car, even with sheets of rain hammering at the windshield. Spunky refuses to disembark—a first.

"Go get that food out there, Spunk, go get it."

The dog stares at me not so dumbly from the warmth and dryness of his backseat kingdom.

"Don't you want to pee on Big Ed, Spunky, don't you want to pee?"

Although Big Ed is spared this golden indignity, after laying a trail of Butcher Bones I finally get the shot. Maybe the rain will taper off around Binghamton, I think, ever (ha ha) hopeful.

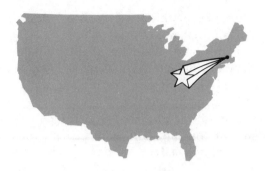

Batting 8th, the Shortstop:
WALTER JAMES VINCENT "RABBIT" MARANVILLE, St. Michael's Cemetery, Springfield, Massachusetts

RABBIT MARANVILLE

Rabbit Maranville rode a cool nickname as far as it can go, hippity-hopping all the way to Cooperstown: he died several months before his induction. No offense to the Bunny Man, but he was the quintessential shortstop, nothing more or less. Of course, that's why we're making this pilgrimage to Springfield.

Rabbit gets his revenge. We drive up on a Sunday; the cemetery office is closed. We pinpoint the section of people who died, like Rabbit, in the mid-'50s: Spunky sniffs out a GARVEY headstone (Thomas), sprinkling lustily on it, but is unable to detect Rabbit. A full day's drive gone to waste? Yes. My girlfriend Julie and her mom have come along for the fun; if it were just me and the Spunk we might search all day, but instead we have to abort the quest and try again tomorrow.

We come back the next day for Rabbit Redux. The harebrained directions we receive at the office are almost no better than none at all, but eventually we detect Rabbit's pale stone. Sometimes a tombstone tells a story; this one's is bittersweet:

Rabbit's accomplishments on the "field of dreamsicles" is unnoted; he is identified only as USNRF, WWI. His first wife, Elizabeth, who died tragically at twenty-three, in the middle of Rabbit's career, is buried beside him. But Rabbit, always a gamer, rallied and married an apparently much younger woman, Helena—no dates are given for her, implying she might still be alive. The simple, unbaseball-y tombstone also implies that Helena, a vital woman, has better things on which to spend the estate.

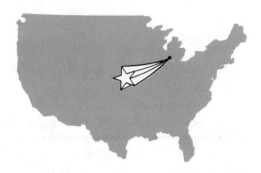

And, batting 9th, the Pitcher:
MORDECAI PETER CENTENNIAL "THREE FINGER" BROWN,
Roselawn Memorial Park, Terre Haute, Indiana

THREE FINGER BROWN

We cross from Kentucky to the southwest Indiana prairie just
before sunset. In Evansville, we pass a Days Inn with a sign reading:
WELCOME IN SEARCH OF EXELLENCE SEMINAR. I've been driving since
Atlanta early this morning, the road is packed and there's nowhere to
make a U-turn, so I have no photo: you'll have to take my word for it.
My second impression of Indiana comes on the outskirts of Terre
Haute, as I hear this motto for a radio station: "Incredible music and
credible news."

I check into a Terre Haute motel, explaining that I have a small,
housebroken pet. The owner, Frank Peterson, glances out and sees

Spunky perched in the driver's seat. "He's sure a cute one," says Frank. He waves to the dog.

HOOOOOOONK! HOOOOOOONK!

Another man checking in behind me, Frank Peterson, asks, "You teach him how to do that?"

Frank the Owner squints suspiciously out at the car, then turns and gives me the old once-over. "I *think* we've got a room. . . ."

HOOOOOOOOOOOOONK!

I dash out to hush the puppy, strapping him to a backseat window crank, then return to the office. Frank the Owner's wife has come out to investigate the commotion. "S'got a trained dog out there," says Frank the Owner, as he warily hands me a key.

Another downside to traveling with my best friend: I always get the room with the prestained carpet.

Mordecai is officially listed in the *Baseball Encyclopedia* under Three Finger Brown. Some speculate that his mangled right hand made him a better pitcher, that he got more dipsy-doodle action as a result, like Tom Dempsey's clubfoot made him such a good football kicker. According to an article by Paul C. Frisz, collected in *Insider's Baseball*, after Brown became famous, even long after he retired to operate a garage in Terre Haute, people still went out to his uncle's farm to view the feed grinder, since stored and polished, that chewed up his hand when he was seven and launched his career.

After Spunky and I visit Three Finger's unadorned ground plaque, we attempt to uncover vestiges or recollections of this wonderful old tourist attraction. Nope: now the town's top draw is the wild and woolly funspot Larry Bird's Boston Connection, featuring the Bird's Nest lounge. The youngsters who extol it sense my disappointment, but have no sympathy for this Charles Kuralt-y fixation on the past. I'm made to feel like the uncoolest guy in Terre Haute. I hate them.

COMPUTATION OF QUEST QUOTIENT

$$QQ = \frac{(M_d/100 + M_f/1000 + P/10 + L/5 + (I \times 10) + D + T) \times DA}{(F/10) + (\$/100) + 1}$$

Mileage driven: $\mathbf{M_d}$ = 3400
Mileage flown: $\mathbf{M_f}$ = 0
Phone calls: $\mathbf{P}$ = 13
Letters: $\mathbf{L}$ = 3
Intimacies: $\mathbf{I}$ = 0
Drop Dead factor: $\mathbf{D}$ = 2
Days spent: $\mathbf{T}$ = 10

Difficulty-Aggravation multiplier: $\mathbf{DA}$ = 2

Failure rate: $\mathbf{F}$ = 0
Cost: $\mathbf{\$}$ = 700

QUEST QUOTIENT = 12.0

☞ *A n a l y s i s :*

Many miles, many days—but almost no difficulty or aggravation on tour. If not for false Yankee start, hard-to-locate Rabbit, and deluge of rain, quest might have had DA of 0 or 1— pure pleasure! Which, of course, has nothing to do with fun.

I NEVER MET A MAC I DIDN'T LIKE . . .

The World's Largest McDonald's

I hate (journalists will tell you not to begin your lead with these two words, but for some reason I come back to them again and again) stories about fast food that take a snide, condescending approach to the subject,

like the author is some gourmet chef in a big hat who dines only at multistar restaurants and regards fast food as plastic, tasteless, and nutritionless, just as do you—he assumes—the reader. What is this, the world-famous French Sorbonne cooking school (you know, where they test various margarines versus butter)?

I don't advocate a diet of *only* burgers, fries, and nuggeted substances, or a ceaseless landscape of franchised homogeneity, but it's a fact that often the best meal in town is at McDonald's, Burger King, Pizza Hut, or Dunkin' Donuts (although if it's Dunkin' Donuts you might ask how far is the next town). When you drive cross-country, naturally you encounter a lot of "strips," and you should be darn glad to have a place where you can get food quickly that will likely be decent—better to be a tasteless, happy American than a snooty connoisseur who died of starvation.

Which brings me to the small town of Vinita, in northeastern Oklahoma. Despite being in the middle of nowhere, Vinita has two superb restaurants: Clanton's Cafe, which serves an exceptional chicken-fried steak, and McDonald's—a McDonald's that is, in fact, the world's largest. Clanton's is closed nights and weekends; besides, if like most travelers here you're zooming past town on the Will Rogers Turnpike, you won't even know it—or Vinita, for that matter—exists. McDonald's, on the other hand, advertises its immense existence for miles in either direction and is easy to spot from the turnpike. You can't miss it, in fact, because the restaurant soars *over* the turnpike, straddling across four lanes and then some: say magnafeek!

I first encountered this palace of fine eats a year prior to my quest, soon after it opened for business and announced its claim to fame. It is one of those places, like a topless car wash or the Grand Canyon, that you never forget. From the outset of this project, I had wanted to include a quest related to fast food, a vital part of my formative years and an intrinsic fact of life on the road. There was never any question but that the Vinita McDonald's would be the ideal place at which to spend some time "behind the arches."

One thing that appeals to me about eating at fast-food restaurants is that it is a noninteractive experience. You don't shoot the breeze with a McDonald's cashier, or ask, "What's good today?" Employees are ritually pleasant, but that's the extent of it. And I like that. Who needs some crapulous Romeo in front of you chatting up the counter gal while you're trying to get fed and back to the office? Individuality breeds inconsistency. I'm not being poetically ironic; roboticness *is* the most efficient policy.

I contact the McDo's home office in Oak Brook, Illinois. If the Vinita outpost is owned and operated by the same corporation that has for years *paid* people to create television commercials featuring an unfunny clown and Barry Manilow music, I will have no chance. Fortunately, however, the world's largest McDonald's is owned by an autonomous franchisee, Ed Silver, who made his gold with the arches in southern Indiana and is now filling Sooner stomachs. Silver, I would later learn, is pretty much a hands-off guy, a seasoned operator who oversees with a keen eye but delegates authority to his deputies, also imported Hoosiers, while he plays golf. He leaves the fate of my quest up to Bill McNeill, his manager.

To my great joy, McNeill, a thirty-one-year-old, thirteen-year McDonald's veteran with a Bachelor of Hamburgerology from Hamburger U., is also pretty independent-minded and not without a sense of humor. He tells me, "Well, we talked it over, and it sounds like a pretty good idea. After all, we consider ourselves sort of a spectacle." I will be joining the crew not for the madhouse summer but for the late winter, professional-travelers-only season.

McNeill greets me and immediately sets me to work on the breakfast crew. In about two seconds I perceive that this team is nothing like the miscreants who infest the McDonald's restaurants back "home" in New York. They treat their work as if it is actually their job, and not some curse brought unjustly down upon them for which the customer must suffer. Employees are eager to show me the ropes; it hasn't quite been explained to them who I am and what I'm doing, but they are willing to obey Bill when he tells them to let me watch for a while and then try it myself.

The restaurant rests on 47 acres, inhabits 29,135 square feet of floor space, and has 300 seats and 400 parking spots. During summer peak, McNeill pays a staff of 166 employees, 90 of whom work each day. It is the world's largest in terms of square footage; according to McNeill, a McDonald's in Guam has the greatest seating capacity. (Yeah, but what are you *eating?*) Amenities include an elevator (the restaurant, bowing over the turnpike as it does, is on the second floor), a conference room, a play area, two gift shops, a travelers' information room, and a huge bank of phones. The McGift Shop sells souvenirs known as McStuff: T-shirts, commander's caps, postcards, etc. McStuff profits, estimated at $40,000 annually, are sent to Ronald McDonald House.

This is the only food service on the turnpike between Joplin, Missouri, and Tulsa (it's halfway between them, not far from the mysterious Tri-State Spooklight), a distance of 114 miles, so the prices—and sales volume—are higher than usual, though hardly extortionate. (Soon after moving here from Indiana, McNeill tells me, they realized they were in a rare and fortuitous "whatever the market will bear" situation; partly as a result, there is little local business, which goes to Clanton's.)

Unlike urban McDonald'ses, which go begging for competent help willing to work at fast-food wages, Vinita's McDonald's is in an enviable position. Management need look no further than the local labor pool, which is small but has only one alternative: the only other part-time employer in the area is a factory, and the pay there is not much better. Conditions here are pleasant—lots of elbow room—and nobody works overtime.

This may seem a sunny (i.e., "z-z-z-z-z") rundown, but the work atmosphere at most fast-food restaurants is tight-quartered, hot, and grimy, and the customers and duties grind you down with their meanness and meniality, respectively—so pardon me if I marvel for a while. There is an esprit de corps here, a pride in the high volume of business and the coolness of being the world's largest. There are also more adult workers here than usual: some are housewives, providing a second income for the family; others, twentyish and easygoing, just haven't found the initiative to move to the big city and land a real job. This might not be a fast track, but the mix does make for a capable crew that would rather serve than sulk.

I am paired with one of the stars, Vicky, who is preparing egg breakfasts. Cooking eggs is one of only two jobs at McDonald's that might potentially yield some human-factor variation. (The other is scooping french fries.) The eggs are all fried together on the grill inside a large metal ring, regardless of how many are being fried at once. When the eggs are ready, the preparer divides them into the proper number of servings—using only her eyeballs to judge portions! I am shocked: this means that no two orders of scrambled eggs will be exactly, precisely alike!

"You get so you can pretty much make 'em all the same," says Vicky.

Yes, but . . . but . . .

An almost Japanese egalitarianism exists here: the staff rotates from station to station throughout the week. Even star employees have to take a turn sweeping the vast parking lot—not a pleasant task in the wind and rain, or when you're a cute young girl being ogled by horny, hopped-up truckers. Each crew member is allowed four dollars' worth of food: a sandwich, fries, drink, and dessert.

Just like the stars and below-pars, it's time for me to rotate. The digital clock ticks toward ten-thirty—time to begin frying up burgers for the lunch menu. I study the names of the three parts of a Big Mac bun: the top is the *crown;* the middle is the *club;* the bottom is the *heel.*

This McDo's has purchased the new "clamshell fryers": instead of an employee needing to flip burgers at the half-cooked stage—a potentially disastrous intrusion of the dreaded human factor—a hinged, heated top comes down atop the burger patty and sears the meat for a prescribed amount of time, depending on the size of the burger, then lifts up automatically. In my opinion, the clamshell fryer is the greatest advance in fast food since the abductable clown head (since eliminated) at Jack-in-the-Box drive-thrus in the '70s. The only problem is wiping the top part of the fryer clean after each use. You scrape with a spatula-type implement that brings your arm—okay, my arm, and it *hurt*—in close proximity to the sizzling 100 percent beef fat.

Next, you assemble the burger. Sandwiches are made in batches, by type; each type has different ingredients. The "bin person" calls out the number and type of sandwiches to be prepared. Special orders are called "grills," and too many grills gum up the system: Burger King's "Hold the pickle/Hold the lettuce/Special orders/ Don't upset us" campaign was pretty well aimed if not quite tuneful.

Also, certain customs only make sense in the context of huge volume and turnover. Fortunately, we Americans are trained for this sort of logic, and only French people ("Zees Weel Rogers—ee eez un rodeo cowboy, *non?* He keel Indians?") and cranky dads with sweat-soaked armpits and floppy hats raise much of a ruckus when their whims are foiled by the exigencies of efficiency. For example, while you *can* get double lettuce on a Big Mac, you can't get *any* lettuce on a quarter-pounder, because quarter-pounders, by "definition," don't come with lettuce.

I move on to the fillet o' fish deep-fryer. The fillet, which is prepared only on command from the bin person, looks like an icy chunk of brown sludge before it's dipped into the fryer. Fillets, McNuggets and french fries are placed in wire baskets and plunged into tubs of oil. A timed beep tells the frying person when to remove them. McNuggets are drained and placed in warming ovens. Fillets o' fish are dripped dry, then assembled in sandwiches.

French fries are dumped into the french-fry bin, where they are salted and scooped into paper or cardboard holders. (If a customer requests no salt, a fresh batch is poured out onto paper towels in the bin. Once again, this special request slows things down drastically.) It's not easy to scoop fries just right: there is an art to making as few fries as possible appear to fill their containers to o'erflowing.

Assistant manager Brian McCoskey, a fourteen-year veteran at the age of twenty-eight, gives me a "good-natured" hard time as he ridicules the way I scoop the fries. It's especially important, he lectures, to make the packages look good. "If customers don't specify a size," he says, "we give 'em large, so we've gotta give 'em a good deal on the large ones. Fries and drinks are the profit items."

Here's a warning: Cholesterol notwithstanding, the most dangerous menu item is the hot fruit pie. According to the manual, pies— with their tongue-scorching filling—require a cooling time of twenty minutes after cooking. A restaurant of this size can afford to keep a few cooled ones always at the ready, but a smaller outlet might be tempted to fry one up on demand and serve it right away. Biter beware!

The aforementioned bin person is the quarterback of the food-preparation process. He decides how much of each item to precook, based on the time of day and the number and girth of awaiting customers. I apprentice at the bin with Todd, a quiet, earnest young man with a great weight on his shoulders: If he orders too much food, the unsold items must be destroyed after eleven minutes. If he is unable to anticipate a sudden need for mass quantities of an item, the entire kitchen is thrown into turmoil.

Todd is a veteran, a true Hero of the Bin. He tells me that truckers, for example, tend to relish the hearty goodness of the quarter-pounder; if Todd glances out the window and sees several semis pulling into the lot, he instinctively orders up a tray or two. I, of course, am not permitted to call out my own orders, but while Todd is preoccupied I take the opportunity to fantasize that I am actually running the show.

The bin person receives the tray of food (the preparer calls, "McDLT's up!," and the b.p. acknowledges, "Thank you!"; back "home," another word is substituted for "thank"), wraps each item, and places it into its slot in the waiting bin, which is heated with moist air—not a heat lamp, as in the old days. Each wrapper is marked with the time its contents should be chucked out. Food stays pretty edible in the bin, but if you're in New York and receive, for instance, a burger marked 23 (for twenty-three minutes after the hour) at forty-five minutes after, you just might want to bring it back, if only to flaunt your inside knowledge. (My pal Mike tried this once in New York and was told that the number was not a time, but a "code." Oh.)

Time to rotate, and my new task is less an amazing riot of fun than those previous. Lori, a friendly young housewife, teaches me how to clean tables. The world's largest McDonald's draws a crowd that is well trained in the McDo's way; they bus their own trays and dump their garbage. I learn the trick of sweeping crumbs from the table onto a tray. Out in the dining area, customers sit before a large semicircular window above the flowing turnpike traffic. A belching tanker truck toots its resonant horn as it passes beneath us. "Truckers do that all the time," explains Lori. "For luck."

The world's largest McDonald's is already a turnpike institution, on every hungry Midwestern motorist's refectory directory: during blizzards, the restaurant might stay open twenty-four hours to accommodate stranded travelers. As a reflection of this synergistic relationship with the turnpike, a directive above the time clock instructs cashiers to give state troopers free meals. Touring celebrities have been known to pay homage to the mighty Mac. Emmylou Harris visited and was reportedly "very nice." B. B. King and Willie Nelson stop by when on tour, although Willie stays in the bus, "meditating."

Because one need not exit the turnpike to eat here, there are parking lots on both sides of the highway. Many a customer, having left the restaurant on the opposite side of which he entered and now unable to locate his car, shrieks that it has been stolen. A manager who has encountered this all too often will chuckle, which does not sit too well with the "victim," and ask him where he was headed, as if that were relevant to a car being stolen, though of course it is. The police no longer take stolen-car complaints seriously here. Thought you might like to know.

Luckily I miss out on bathroom-cleaning detail. The environs seem fairly spiffy, but Bill admits that in the Spring Blitz, during which McDonald's stores were rated competitively on cleanliness, the world's largest McDonald's was an also-ran (although by New York City standards the world's largest McDonald's seems like an operating room). The year 1989, it must be noted, was Clean Bathrooms Year for McDonald's. Did you notice?

It is 11 P.M. Through the picture windows we can see some heavy weather moving in across the Oklahoma flatness—a blizzard. The restaurant must remain open until midnight, then workers spend another half-hour closing. The youthful night shift is worrying about getting home, as a steady rain is solidifying to sleet and beyond. I assess my options: journalistically, it might be neat to experience some emergency conditions, maybe even spend the night here. But as a tired little soldier, I would rather cut out early—writer's prerogative—and head back to my motel to catch an R-rated movie before the roads are impassable. See ya' tomorrow, kids.

The next morning, the streets of Vinita, normally tranquil anyway, are soundless, blanketed with ice. Gloveless and numb, I use my Swiss army knife to chip the Dodge Shadow, encased like Lenin, out of its glacial shroud. There are no other guests at the motel. Me and my Shadow creep slowly to McDonald's—no sign of life on the five-mile route from the motel to the turnpike. The restaurant, however, is abuzz with travelers; truckers huddle over coffee in the TV area scoping the Weather Channel. The contrast between the world of the interstate and the town it passes is vivid: despite their proximity, one has nothing to do with the other. Driving the interstate, one has about as much connection with the land as one does in a plane flying over. So what? There's nothing wrong with that: at least on the interstate you can anticipate how long it will take to get where you're going—and there are bathrooms, too, unlike on the "blue highways."

I don my staff garb and hunker down to work. After paying my dues—unloading a truck, rotating heavy stock in the slippery meat lockers, dragging out heaps of garbage—I am almost ready to work the cash register, or, in McDo parlance, to be a "window person." Bills tells me that until I started carting oozing bags of rubbish, many of his staff thought I was a spy from the company because of my haircut. He asks me to watch an instructional video that drills home the six-step process of working the window (see THE SIX STEPS).

Bill sits and chats as I watch the video. I confess to him that I am impressed with his operation—not only with its size but also with the unimperious way that he and the other managers relate to the employees. I note, however, a disparity between the day shift and the night shift. The night crew seems more offhandedly assured, quicker at their duties and with their wits. "Yes," he says. "The day shift has a lot of second-income people and . . . well, losers; on the night shift we have a lot of young, sharp kids." One explanation is that most of the night workers have something else moving forward in their lives —school, or perhaps another job.

There is a career track at McDonald's, but it's long and, until one moves into management, excruciatingly low-paying. After one becomes a manager, the next step is either to get noticed by the company and be offered a job as a supervisor, or get what is called a BFL loan from the company to open your own store. Once the loan is approved, and a store assigned, the owner must attend an intensive two-week course at Hamburger U., in Oak Brook, as well as completing a workbook that takes three months. All owners *must* attend: the company does not want uncommitted investors. If you just want to invest, they figure, you can buy McDonald's stock.

I take my place at the counter with Patrick, another star employee. I am about to fulfill a lifelong fantasy: I'm going to take someone's order at McDonald's. It is late afternoon, time for snacks and ice cream. My first order, from an adorable little girl, is for a soft-serve cone. Since I have never encountered a soft-serve machine at any McDonald's that didn't dispense a gloppy mess, I regard this as a call to adventure. And sure enough, the soft-serve *is* a little on the repugnant side. But, darn it, Patrick adjusts something and, after I toss two in the garbage, my third cone comes out looking presentable.

Working the window goes very much the way I always dreamed it would. The customers know exactly what they want, and none of them demand a word of extraneous conversation; by my very stance behind the counter of McDonald's, I possess a shell of impersonality that no one attempts to pierce. Of course, as I said, this is not a local hangout; people come in here to get food and get going. Their presence on the turnpike indicates a certain desire for alacrity. My stint is a success in that it is prototypical.

I retreat to the employees' lounge to check out some of the other training videos, which are pretty entertaining for aficionados of heavy-handed mind control. The background music features perky but fore-boding minor chords, cueing the viewer to be alert and happy but to beware because *the unexpected* might happen at any time. As in a TV commercial, the employee-actors are zitlessly attractive. In the videos, problems are something to look forward to, because they are "special service opportunities."

In *Customer Service and the Disabled Customer*, an employee who hasn't seen this video and hasn't dealt much with the disabled attempts to give "special treatment" to a disabled person; the cripple snaps at her nastily for her condescension. There's some nice tension here. *The Competitive Edge*, shown to new employees, is mostly about a runner in training, and seems like a Nike commercial. Then it somehow cuts to the Ray Kroc story (he made McDo's what it is today, and the San Diego Padres too, but you can't win 'em all), then draws a parallel to you, the crew. At the end, the runner wins the big race and you become the best crew person you can possibly be.

Also worth renting are *A Study in Breakfast, Pts. 1 and 2, Lot and Lobby, Dress Procedures* (about dressing food—a pun, maybe), and *It Only Takes One Time. One Time*, for managers, is about security; it's very scary, with the tone of an infomercial, or "America's Most Wanted." In this one, a three-piece-suited secret service type narrates a simulated robbery, in which a window girl is manhandled by armed thugs. We are told that when locking up for the night, we should check out the false ceilings in the bathrooms, because criminals will hide up there until closing, then crawl over to the manager's office, jump down, and plunder the safe. This seems farfetched to me, but I later learn that this is indeed a popular technique for burglars who have learned well the story of the Trojan horse. (Ha ha, in that case maybe they should hide in the condom machine.)

All too soon it's time to say goodbye. (By the way, you won't find condom machines at McDonald's; that was just a hilarious pun.) Before I go, Bill informs me, in an almost apologetic "Son, your mother and I are getting a divorce" tone, that he will be moseying on down the road in the near future: he, Brian, Ed Silver, and comanager Jim Criswell will be selling out and taking over four stores in the Musko-gee, Oklahoma, area, a town with a nowhereness made famous by the

Merle Haggard song "Okie from Muskogee." Still, compared to depressing Vinita, Muskogee must seem as hustly-bustly as Tokyo during a Hypertensive Chain Smokers convention. For Bill and his family, it is, as he says, "a quality of life issue."

On my way out the door, I figure I might as well ask a few of the "tough" questions. Bill is a good guy, and might be willing to divulge a McSecret or two. "Have there been any *hushed-up* incidents at McDonald's? You know, mass food poisonings, more San Ysidro–type massacres that they managed to cover up, Ronald pulling his pants down, Rat McNuggets . . . ?"

"Could very well be. But I've never heard any of it."

So much for that. Bill tells me his dream, a dream that draws many behind the golden arches, a dream that will very likely come true for him. "I can tell you're not too money-motivated," he says. "Now, that's okay. Me, I am money-motivated. I want to retire as a millionaire by the time I'm forty." (Brian earlier told me *he* was going to be a millionaire by the age of thirty-five.)

Bill praises my work and kindly offers me—I hope he was serious —a job in Muskogee. Now, if I were more money-motivated I might . . . nah.

The Six Steps

(FROM THE INSTRUCTIONAL VIDEOTAPE COUNTER 1: THE SIX STEPS)

1) Greet the customer. "Hello, welcome to McDonald's. May I take your order?" (Vary the greeting. You don't want to sound like a robot.)
2) Take the order and suggestive sell or sell-up. "Would you like fries with that?" "Will that be *large* fries?" *Never* suggest to children.
3) Assemble the order.
4) Present the order. Food and fries in middle, drinks on right, dessert on left.
5) Receive payment. Put bill face down on drawer as you give change. (There have been cases of felons pasting twenties over ones on bills; hard to tell looking at picture side.)
6) Thank customer and ask for repeat business. "Thanks. And come again."

COMPUTATION OF QUEST QUOTIENT

$$QQ = \frac{(M_d/100 + M_f/1000 + P/10 + L/5 + (I \times 10) + D + T) \times DA}{(F/10) + (\$/100) + 1}$$

Mileage driven: M_d = 400
Mileage flown: M_f = 2700
Phone calls: P = 5
Letters: L = 2
Intimacies: I = 0
Drop Dead factor: D = 0
Days spent: T = 5

Difficulty-Aggravation multiplier: DA = 7

Failure rate: F = 0
Cost: $\$$ = 600

QUEST QUOTIENT = 12.6

☞ *Analysis:*

Thought this would rate higher, with promising DA multiplier going in, 8 or 9 possible. But difficulty subsided the instant I got the okay; if not for getting snowbound on drive to Oklahoma City in perilous blizzard, boosting aggravation, DA might have been as low as 5. . . . Flying instead of driving to Tulsa cost crucial mileage points.

Please Stand
_By_

y pal Mike Wilkins and I have long felt a desire to spend a year generating false news stories and phony press releases in an attempt to create a small pocket of chaos, to force a re-evaluation of fact-gathering processes in a stagnant, self-righteous media climate—and to have fun. We reached this diagnosis after an experimental series of trial balloons—humor pieces, book and story ideas, screenplays, treatments, and the like—were ruthlessly punctured via form letter, without due consideration, by pompous gatekeepers of dubious mentality.

Unfortunately, this idea, too, required approbation, in the form of a book advance: we'd need to establish phone lines in several cities, and there would also be the expenses of printing, photos, stationery, mail drops, and probably a lawyer. Again, the publishing cartel was blind to the urgency of our mission.

Mike got discouraged, returned to Stanford for his MBA, and became an investment banker, merging banks by day and conducting an exhaustive study of Japanese animated monster-porn by night. I kept plodding away in my inert fashion, came up with the idea for this book, and received a tidy advance.

Moderately sanctioned now, I decide it would certainly be in the *American Quest* spirit to pull off, with Mike's collaboration, at least *one* hoax. We begin to sift through our bag of ideas for a few that could be done inexpensively.

Before we have time to proceed, I receive a call from a researcher at *Harper's* magazine regarding a totally and, I thought, *obviously* fictitious humor piece I wrote for *Premiere* magazine several months earlier about strange video collectors, people who accumulate and swap such mundane and ludicrous video ephemera as test patterns, FBI warnings, and closed-circuit department store surveillance tapes. Although the article is subtitled "Mind-numbing antics not to be believed," this caveat goes unheeded.

This Harperian is interested in possibly excerpting, in a section of the magazine called Readings, a newsletter mentioned in the piece, one I had posited for "humorous" purposes, entitled *Please Stand By*. The idea is that there is an organized cult of nutballs out there who spend all their time monitoring TV, waiting for technical difficulties (known as TDs) to occur, videotaping the proceedings, and swapping the tapes with other cultists—one of them, I had written, even publishes this newsletter.

Now, I might inform the researcher that *Please Stand By* does not exist, and that it is a joke. But my mind flashes back two years to my second rejection letter from *Harper's* editor Lewis Lapham. The first time I was rejected, you see, I had naively thought that Lapham's quirky syntax indicated that I was receiving a personal note, not just a form rejection. This, to a writer, is tantamount to outright acceptance. But the second rejection, which I achieved a year later, was almost identical to the first: my fool's paradise was toppled in a bloody coup. I want payback and, instead of my having to search it out, here it is, downstairs in the lobby, buzzing my apartment and asking to be let in.

I alert Mike—who these days is helping independent banks and savings institutions realize maximum value for their shareholders through a multifaceted program intended to increase stock liquidity, unlocking upside potential sequestered by a temporarily inefficient market—to the situation and ask if he'd be interested in becoming the "editor" of *Please Stand By.* Yes, he says, not in so many words.

I give *Harper's* Mike's phone number and his *nom de scam,* Ian Michaels. (He chooses this name because it sounds so suave.) "Ian" tells the researcher that he is very excited she called, and, coincidentally, he is right this minute preparing the "latest" issue—he'll ship it next week.

With the help of a Macintosh and a few pals, Stefan Hammond and Jim Morton, Ian creates and publishes *Please Stand By* for only sixty dollars. In his conversations with representatives of the jerky-kneed intellectual monthly (*Harper's*—not *Please Stand By,* which is, ostensibly, a quarterly), Ian senses a disguised taunting: clearly they consider him some kind of cretin, and they are going to have a jolly old time holding him up to national ridicule. Mike and I know the symptoms well; we have done it ourselves once or twice. But we don't allege our work to be *sensitive* or *important; Harper's,* which ostensibly reprints items out of context not to poke fun—an *honorable* motive—but to lead you to your own judgments, does.

Soon after Mike FedExes *Please Stand By* to *Harper's,* a serendipitous news item appears in *The New York Times:* it seems a hilarious spoof that *Harper's* (!) ran in 1981, a supposed "new find" in the realm of Freudian scholarship, was accepted as legitimate by several Vandyke-wearing pointy-heads, and had been scrutinized and cited in their further research. Whoops! "*Harper's* as well as Professor Gay [the spoof's author] has some explaining to do," a certain indignant and red-faced Professor Crews is quoted as whining. "*Harper's* has traditionally been more literary than scholarly," countered Lapham. "We deal in irony and many other literary devices."

Everything seems to be falling into my lap in this quest (too bad the same isn't true of my Kiss Ten '60s TV Sirens quest, if you know what I mean), and now I am given a bogus but apparently very real sense of purpose. "Yes," I can say, probably without sniggering, "I have hoisted *Harper's* on its own petard. The outraged community of gullible Freudian scholars, of which I consider myself a spiritual guardian, has been vindicated at last."

After the excerpts—edited for clarity, brevity, and grammar, but apparently never checked for veracity—run in the June *Harper's*, Mike-Ian receives a frantic call from his contact there: a television station in Duluth, Minnesota, has been scandalized by a mention in *Please Stand By*'s Sightings section, reprinted in *Harper's*, of a technical difficulty that they claim never happened. (The station, WDIO, was misidentified for humorous purposes in *PSB* as KDIO):

> 11/23/88—KDIO, Duluth, Minnesota
> Right at the beginning of the ten o'clock KDIO newscast, the center camera zoomed in on the female news anchor's lips to focus. It didn't zoom out. The camera tilted rapidly down toward the floor. When they switched to another camera you could see the other news anchor, his face contorted with anger, screaming, "I don't know WHAT the hell is going on!" and tossing his papers in the air and walking off the set. They immediately cut to the station's PLEASE STAND BY slate, which shows a bearded Viking in a horned helmet sadly watching a malfunctioning television set. Great!! (Reported by Dave Lundquist, Hibbing, Minnesota.)

A research at Harper's calls Mike to inform him that WDIO is threatening legal action, presumably since propagation of this misinformation might have serious ramifications on something or other. (Interestingly, the station's logo is indeed a bearded Viking in a horned helmet.) What the researcher wants to know is, Do you have proof, my good friend Ian, that this did occur?

"Ho-boy," replies an incredulous Ian, "I'd be really surprised if it didn't. That TD was reported by Dave Lundquist, and he's usually very reliable. I'll ask him to check his video library, and I'll get back to you."

Ian waits a few days, then calls *Harper's*. "You know, this has really strained my relationship with Dave Lundquist," he says. "We had a big argument. It was *another* station that had the technical difficulty." He offers to print a retraction in the next issue of *Please Stand By*.

Meanwhile, Ian receives several more calls from the media regarding *Please Stand By*. A Miami TV producer wants to do a story on the organization. Can Ian send him some sample TD tapes? Why, suuuure! Ian scavenges together a bawdy collection of satellite-feed bloopers, such as a sparsely attended football game at which a woman orally pleases her male companion under a blanket. Ian never hears back from the man.

Ian also fields about a dozen calls from *Harper's* readers who want to join the cult. (*Harper's* advertisers, please take note: is this the audience you were promised?) One caller, however, puts Mike's ethics to the test.

Andy Meisler, from *California* magazine, wants to do a story on *PSB:* this would be a great break for us. He asks Ian, however, if this is "for real." It isn't fair or funny to perpetuate a hoax if its authenticity is questioned; after all, we're trying to nail those who would parasitically jump on *PSB* as a cheap butt of humor, those who would pigeonhole this cult as consisting of a bunch of moronic TV viewers without giving any credence at all to the possibility that the creators of *PSB* might possibly be as ultraclever as themselves. Besides, Meisler is the "as told to" coauthor (with Cynthia Garvey) of the delightful *Secret Life of Cyndy Garvey.* So Ian demurs, explaining he doesn't want publicity that might make fun of himself and his friends.

In August, *Harper's* prints what *Spy* magazine, which gleefully chronicles the tale because *Spy* is embroiled in a bit of unrelated professional crossfire with *Harper's,* terms a "not entirely correct correction":

> "[A] Readings excerpt from *Please Stand By* . . . described a botched newscast that was followed immediately by a PLEASE STAND BY sign picturing a bearded Viking. The Viking was, in fact, the symbol of television station WDIO-TV in Duluth, but the technical difficulty occurred on another station."

After the *Spy* article appears in September, I am told that "all hell is breaking loose" at *Harper's.* Items for the Readings section are being scrutinized with more care than ever (see Freddie Prinze Commemorative Stamp quest). A limp correction appears in the November 1989 issue:

> "The June 1989 issue of *Harper's Magazine* included a Readings excerpt from *Please Stand By,* which was described as a quarterly newsletter about 'technical difficulties' on television. It has recently been brought to the editors' attention that the 'newsletter' was spurious."

"Newsletter"? Spurious? Hahahahahahahaha.

PLEASE STAND STAND STAND BY

Vol. 3
No. 4
Winter 1988

VIDEO SIMULACRA: A MELDING OF TECHNICAL DIFFICULTIES AND THE IMAGINATION
By Sheila Duignan

A rock formation that resembles an elephant. The back of a moth that appears to be the menacing face of an owl. A ginseng root shaped like a man. These are just a few of the better known examples of "simulacra," those objects with likenesses of, or resemblances to, other objects. And usually the resemblance is of a living thing. Everyone is aware of such objects. Old Man Rock in The White Mountains of New Hampshire is one. The various reports of the head of Christ on tortillas, refrigerators, and in the grain of wooden hospital doors are others. What many people don't know about are "video simulacra," images which appear during a technical difficulty, after the station has signed-off for the evening (without a test pattern), or when the receiver is far away from the transmitter. These are not as widely reported by the media as other simulacras, though they used to be.

In the early days of the medium of TV, video simulacra were given a good deal of press coverage. The reasons for this included: More viewer reports of simulacras then than now (more viewers were fascinated enough by their new piece of furniture to watch a snowy blank set, and were therefore more likely to notice a simulacra), public curiosity and lack of understanding about television, less programming (more opportunity to watch snow), and less technical expertise (more breakdowns at home and at the station). In the San Francisco area, for example, local papers reported at least 7 video simulacra between 1952 and 1953. These ranged from "rattlesnakes," to a "dog jumping in rhythm," to a "helmeted Nazi." A whole neighborhood showed up to watch Mr. & Mrs. E. Ferguson's "Philco, where she was tuning in the head and torso of a heavy-set man, alternately waving and motioning to be set free." The "Noe Valley Snowman" returned to The Ferguson's Philco for 7 straight days, and became a local celebrity in the process.

As programming filled more and more dead hours, as initial technical problems were solved, and as the novelty of TV as thing wore off, less reports of video simulacra were mentioned in the newspapers. But that is no reason to think that they stopped happening. One of The San Francisco Technical DiffiCult's older members, Peter Wirth, had a group of friends during the 60's who would watch dead air in search of simulacra. Says Wirth, "Better was a channel, like Channel 3, that had no local broadcaster using it, but which had a user in Sacramento or Santa Rosa. Late at night, when the ionosphere had calmed down, we'd start to get these fuzzy images. I call them technical difficulties because if the technology of our receiver, or of their transmitter, was better, we'd have gotten a clearer picture. You really had to use your imagination. Pretty soon, you'd start to see things, patterns at first, then creatures, some you could tell were lions or squids, but others you didn't know what they were, only that they seemed to be alive. Sometimes we saw religious icons. But I was always amazed at how much we were in agreement about what it was, exactly, that we were watching."

Religious video simulacra, as we know, are still reported. The image of a weeping Christ appearing on sets in the Oklahoma panhandle, which residents claimed warned of an approaching tornado. The fuzzy photograph (yet to be verified by a photo lab) of a crucifixion scene, seemingly sharing the screen with the old gameshow, Split-Second. And, most recently, the "Snowy Madonna" of Sandoval County, New Mexico [See "Station Break", of PSB, Spring, 1988 - Ed.] Pilgrims from as far away as Washington State made the trip to the Esquelo farm to see this "miracle." The set was left on continually for three weeks until local church officials, fearing the bad publicity associated with photos of their parishioners setting their sick children in front of an old TV set (which did happen), said that it was not a miracle and asked that the Esquelo's set be turned off.

If video simulacras are not miracles, what are they? Most are of fleeting duration, and could be caused by almost anything from storms to low-flying planes to a neighbor's electric razor. A few are long-lasting (like The Esquelo's), and may be due to a defect in the TV set itself. But is anything really there?

The poet Artaud visited Mexico in the 30's, and found that certain images repeated themselves, in rocks, on trees, in animals. "The land," he wrote in The Peyote Dance, "is full of signs, forms and natural effigies which in no ways seem the result of chance. [It is] as if the Gods themselves had chosen to express their powers by means of these strange signatures." To see "the whole world in a grain of sand," to believe that everything contains a reflection of the universe, is an idea that goes back at least as far as the medieval Doctrine of Signatures, and in some metaphysical sense this is what video simulacra are. It is not in the prejudiced mirror of TV programming that television contains its best reflection of the human condition. It is rather, perhaps, in the impressionist static of a technical difficulty that man, by seeing what he believes to be there sees more accurately his own beliefs. Video simulacra are a truer cast from the anvil of worldy experience and the hammer of reason than the pressed plastic trivets extruded by Hollywood.

STATION BREAK

Welcome, TD'ers. Thanks for your patience with my delay in getting out the Winter PSB, but in addition to the time demands of the holiday season, our "Tightly knit band of loosely knit buds" has grown by leaps and bounds, and it is harder to keep up with all of you. The big news is that we will be featured in an upcoming issue of Premier Magazine in a story written by Jack Bart about different video collector societies. Premier is national, so you should be able to find it in your local newsstand. Also heartening is both the number of letters coming in, and the geographical diversity of where they are coming from. For the third straight issue, I have received more good letters than could fit in PSB. Maybe its time to go to bi-monthly? I'll need help, though.

A number of new members have asked for shortcuts to finding and recording TD's. Such a request, I know, is sending shivers of cold bile through old members who feel that the long hours of waiting and scanning before finally connecting with a juicy glitch gives real thrill to the process. So many things, these days, are done for us that it is hard to find something that gives one a genuine sense of accomplishment when the job is finally completed. With TD'ing, there is a real chance that you will try for days, and still not find that "Crack in the greasepaint" (TV Critic Michael Arlen). That you cannot produce a TD on demand, or just walk to the local 7-11 and buy one is the hobby's attraction for many intrepid viewers. When you finally capture one on tape, it's completely yours (But please share your find - another pleasure). And as most of us will tell you, nothing beats that feeling.

Still there are some hints for those that want to get their feet wet without having to go on "solo safari."

1): Technical difficulties tend to come in bundles. Oftentimes, the cause of the TD, be it human, natural, or phantom, is of long duration, and once one TD occurs, another caused by the same problem can be forthcoming quickly. If you're scanning and catch the tail-end of a breakdown, hold it there, set up your VCR and wait. Be patient. It's like being in a duck blind and seeing a lone duck. Don't worry,

Continued on page 6

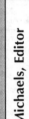

By Ian Michaels, Editor

LETTERS

Dear PSB:

A friend gave me your booklet, and I would like to receive more in the mail. I am glad to know there are others out there like me, especially now that I am retired. I have two TVs on tables next to each other in my living room. I look for mistakes during programs, rather than in between them. Like the time a newswoman for WRAL [*the CBS affiliate in Raleigh, NC - Ed.*] was standing on the street in front of a bunch of kids talking about juvenile crack use, and she said "Back To You, Charlie [*WRAL's anchorman Charlie Gaddy - Ed.*]," and nothing happens so that she still has to keep standing there and the kids start waving even more and start grabbing for her microphone. You could hear their hands hitting against it. I taped that one, if other people are interested in swapping. I am interested in collecting tapes of when sportscasters read scores and highlights from one sport when videotape from another sport is played by accident. I also have made boxes for holding more than one remote control device at a time. These are for sale or trade. Keep up the good work.

Sincerely,
Scott Robinson
Durham, NC

Dear Editor:

I disagree that the four examples you cited in "Frightening Difficulties" [*PSB , Summer, 1988]* are actually the most frightening technical glitches ever broadcast. I recall one from about 15 years ago on a Philadelphia station that tops them all. It was about 2 in the afternoon, during a commercial break and the familiar EBS "test" announcement came on. You know: "For the next sixty seconds...This is only a test," followed by that annoying 1 KHz tone. Well, the tone just keeps going and going, one, two, maybe five minutes. Then the tone stops and the picture glitches and there's nothing but snow. The snow is going for maybe sixty seconds. My first thought was 'Jesus, this is no test, this is an actual emergency, a nuclear hit on Philly's Naval shipyard that took all the broadcast towers in Center City with it.' I finally switched to another channel, and was relieved to see normal programming. This particular TD greatly influenced my decision to support the anti-nuclear movement. I'm sure you can see why. Your readers might want to think about that the next time someone questions them about the validity of our particular hobby.

Sincerely,
Ken Smith
Harrison, NJ

Dear PSB:

The engineers in Sun Microsystems' Flamingo group love your newsletter...some of them have even started collecting TD material on their own! We were wondering, though, if technical difficulties noticeable only by broadcast engineers or EE's warrant mention in PSB. Those guys can run various broadcasts through a vectorscope and waveform monitor. You'd be surprised at how often stations, even network affiliates, roll off a VHF transient, <u>without time-base correction</u>, and most people

think it's just crappy reception. Cable suppliers can be even worse, but these are usually line level problems and it would be hard to actually prove anything "in court." Perhaps you'd be interested in a regular column on these sorts of issues?

Sineing Off,
Jeff Wilkins
San Carlos, CA

Dear PSB:

I have a nifty trick I like to pass on to other TD-ers. As we all know, the toughest part of our hobby is that you never know when a technical difficulty will occur, or on what channel. I don't know about most of you, but I can't afford to video tape every channel 24 hours a day — why here in Denver, we have dozens of cable stations and that means I'd need dozens of VCRs — Ha! So what I did was buy lots of old teevee sets and stack them up like a store. Now, when I see a technical difficulty, I quickly tune the VCR to that station and let her roll. The only problem is I miss the first few seconds that are often the best. And also I have to watch the teevee more than the average Neilsen family. But I love it. Your magazine, too.

Sincerely,
Leslie Leland
Golden, CO

Dear PSB:

An interesting TD happened here late last year during an electrical storm. I was watching a rerun of "Mork 'n Mindy" when I heard a big crack of lightning. Suddenly the TV started making weird noises just when Mork [*played, of course, by TD collector Robin Williams - Ed.*] was supposed to be talking in a funny voice. He sounded like a spaceman for sure. Any other TDers up here in the Inland Empire?

Go for it,
Cody Peck
Spokane, WA
[*Cody: See New Clubs Column. - Ed.*]

Dear PSB:

In college I spent a semester interning at a local public access cable station that ran four hours of religious programming every Sunday morning. The shows ranged from local evangelists proselytizing to an imaginative puppet show featuring three apostles and a whale. The simplest solution to "Please Stand By" situations (which occurred quite frequently) was to go to a framed portrait of Christ, without any audio, titles or explanation of any kind. Sometimes this image would sit on the screen for as long as fifteen minutes. Apparently the thinking was that the kind of people watching this programming would be perfectly content to look at Jesus. Perhaps some of them said a prayer for us, or saw it as another sign of the Apocalypse. I'd be interested in hearing from other readers about religious oriented technical difficulties.

Doug Kirby
Middletown, NJ

ARE SCRAMBLED CABLE SIGNALS *REALLY* TECHNICAL DIFFICULTIES?

YES! By Jim Morton

Scrambled Signals Deserve A Look!

First, let's define our terms. Scrambled signals mean any signals that are purposely distorted so that some segment of the viewing audience is excluded from watching. TD's are anything that occurs to change the way a show is intended by its creators (producers/writers/directors) before it is seen by its ultimate audience. If these definitions are accepted, then scrambled signals are TD's, Q.E.D. The creators of RoboCop, The Untouchables, or even Police Academy IV certainly did not intend to have their audience get seasick watching their movies, screen rolling, "hitting the beach."

This begs the real question, of course, one that is fundamental to our pursuit: Why do we enjoy a technical difficulty? As I see it, there are two answers - which is why this debate is taking place. One view, surely the one my esteemed colleague espouses, is that the fun in TD's comes precisely from knowing that it was not planned like scrambled signals. A planned TD is a paradox. That the scrambled signal is just what the cable moguls want to send out reduces its fascination. So what, we think, a soon to be sacked engineer hasn't just spilled coffee over a patch board, destroying the organization of information sent skyward. Rather, the causer of this scrambled signal probably got promoted, helping the fat corporate cats squeeze ever more money out of an entertainment-happy populus. I must admit to some sympathy for this line of thought.

BUT, it really is a narrow view of things. Many find, myself included, that TD's *qua* TD's are beautiful. Beautiful even stripped of the baggage of intentionality. This view agrees, yes, an unintentional TD is interesting and funny - so are scrambled cable signals!

Spend an evening watching scrambled Playboy Channel. I find it both avant-garde and arousing in a way that would make Naim June Pak jealous. This is super video art! The pink and orange tones of what must be beautiful bodies roll past, then a picture snaps on clearly, only a-ha, with the sky red, the bodies blue, and the pounding ocean purple. Sound comes and goes in bites, adding its own erotic punctuation.

Watch for several nights, and you start being able to mentally unscramble the picture. You can decipher the intensity of movement, pink to non-pink ratio, and a rough count on the number of limbs in shot. Yes, this scrambling of signal is done on purpose, but the interaction of phase problem and program make for unintentional and unexpected combinations, a feast for the eyes. Not as funny as an incorrectly cued commercial, perhaps, but definitely more evocative.

Our hobby is big enough for two different world views. Scrambled cable signals deserve to be called TD's.

NO! By David N. Brewster

Scrambled signals are *not* TD!

On the subject of scrambled signals, I beg to differ with my colleague. I am of the opinion that scrambled television signals can never aspire to the realm of TD.

The basis of my argument is simple. Any "junior technician" with a modified time base corrector or Marantz SX–20 waveshaper can invert a horizontal or vertical sync pulse and play havoc with an NTSC signal. We've all heard stories about somebody with a homebuilt Tesla coil taking out the whole block on Super Bowl Sunday. Video companies try to figure out ever–increasingly sophisticated methods of copy–protection for their tapes (and some are pretty sneaky too!).

So, where does the avid TD collector draw the line? HBO has been scrambling their satellite signal full–time since '84; does that mean I have to own all that footage on top of everything else? Sheesh, I can barely get into the ol' video vault as it is (re-catalogued last week and can't find anything, natch). I mean, some of the scrambling schemes are pretty interesting— especially Wrestlemania II (1986) and Spinks/Tyson with that wicked Every–Seven–Minutes subcarrier shift (1987)—but I hardly think that scrambled ESPN signals constitute collectible TD (especially since Gayle Gardner went to NBC. Shame on you, ESPN!). What about Movie Channel and Cinemax? How many distorted, jumping copies of Arthur II and Jaws: The Revenge do you have to collect before you scream: "Enough is enough! Scrambled signals are *not* TD!!!"???

TD has contributed its share to the video universe, without question. Some of the legendary tidbits—Sam Donaldson yanking the earphone out of his ear in 1981, the 1958 Cleveland Indian Head Pattern, Curt Gowdy's 1976 World Series "Whoopsie!" incident, and of course, the infamous 1972 F.Y. Charlie—have even been getting attention in the mainstream video press (but not enough!). To sully this select group of video collectibles with the inclusion of "scrambling" just doesn't make any sense to me. Everybody loves scrambles. I don't think there's a collector on the planet who doesn't get a little excited when that dish picks up a scrambled signal and the waveform monitor starts looking like a Mixmaster on high speed! Maybe it's a secret transmission from the Pentagon, or the KGB, or Mars (till we tweak it down and find out it's only "Bombay Broadcast Network" or some such; HAW!). It's always fun, and a challenge. But to elevate this stuff to the level of TD is, in my view, absurd.

SIGHTINGS

A selection of the best sightings sent in by cult cats and lone wolves from around the country. Not all sightings are used in this column, but all are logged. If your sighting does not appear in PSB, do not be discouraged, and please continue to report. A complete sighting log for the years 1983-1988 will be available by summer. NOTE: Please give as much catalog-style information as possible. This includes: Date and time of incident, originating channel's # and city, guilty parties, etc. We are still not getting this basic info for a number of sightings.

10/2/88   CNN, Cable
During 2:00 AM EDT weatherbreak, weatherperson could not figure out where she was in relation to the map behind her. Kept pointing at Great Lakes as if they were the Great Plains.
Reported by PSB STAFF, San Francisco, CA

10/20/88   Home Shopping Club, Cable
4:30 PM EDT. Electronic Flea Collar offered for sale caused audio feedback on host's line. Problem solved by pair of hands coming on camera and switching off collar.
Reported by JIM MORTON, San Francisco, CA

10/30/88   KTRK, Houston, TX
Live reporter doing story on city's various Halloween preparations for 10:00 PM news was wearing a blue shirt, making his head and hands appear to float above his torso. Didn't tape it because at first we thought it was purposely ghoulish. But halfway through his story, the video portion of his remote was stopped, and station cut back to an earlier slide of a jack-o-lantern carved to look like Michael Dukakis.
Reported by GLITCH HOUNDS, Houston, TX.

11/05/88   WTTW, Chicago, IL
More pledge break problems for this educational channel. Last November's pledge week was a feast for us Windy City TD'ers. During breaks in The Singing Detective, camera cues were mixed up four times in a row: those talking were not on camera for more than a minute straight. Those shown but not knowing they were on air included a row of Shrine Clowns glumly looking at their phones, and an auction board assistant tugging at her skirt. Was that "Sh*t!" & "God-damned!" we heard in the background?
Reported by CHICAGOLAND GANG, Niles, IL.

11/08/88   WBAL, Baltimore, MD &
**   WRC, Washington, DC**
Both stations are NBC affiliates. Often, the two are showing the same programs, sometimes with a several second delay from each other. Some areas can receive both stations. During the broadcast of Matlock(apr. 8:20 PM) sync-pulse problems, probably caused by trunk interference, occurred with WRC's signal, and a wonderful tape was made by going back and forth between channels - five seconds of garbled signal, then five seconds of the same stuff clear, then back (missing five seconds of the show in the process, of course).

It's hilarious trying to guess what's happening using the distorted image, then seeing just how wrong you were with the clear image. Others in the capital area might want to check this anomaly out for their own amusement.
Reported by DAVE SAHLIN, Arlington,, VA.

11/09/88   KTVU, Oakland, CA
Only one camera working on Two At Noon for a few minutes. You could hear people in the background trying to fix broken camera, and working camera had to pan back and forth between anchors. Fixed after commercial.
Reported by SNOW BUNNIES, San Francisco, CA.

11/18/88   CNN, Cable
Same episode of Sanford & Son ran on both Thursday & Friday (7:35 PM, EST)
Reported by MANY.

11/23/88   KDIO, Duluth, MN
The local news in the Duluth/Superior area is always mother–lode territory for TD prospectors, this is one of the best: Right at the beginning of the Ten O'clock KDIO newscast, the center camera zoomed in on the female newsanchor's lips to focus. They didn't zoom out; the camera tilted rapidly down toward the floor. Switching to another camera showed the other newsanchor, his face contorted with anger, screaming "I don't know WHAT the hell is going on!," tossing his papers in the air and walking off the set. They immediately cut to the KDIO "Please Stand By" slate, which shows a bearded Viking with horned helmet sadly watching a malfunctioning television set. Great!!
Reported by Dave Lundquist, Hibbing, MN

11/23/88   Channel 12 , Tijuana, MX
This Mexican channel, whose signal is seen in San Diego, ran People's Court video, but with the audio translation track from Divorce Court. Muy divertente. [No call letters given - Ed.]
Reported by Perry Vasquez, La Jolla, CA

SIGHTINGS SCORECARD: SEP-NOV, 1988

TYPE		LOCATION	
IntraStudio, Technical:	51	Universal:	31
IntraStudio, Personality:	41	Network:	16
Transmission, Technical:	19	Cable/Superstation:	26
Transmission, Natural:	25	Local:	62
Set Specific:	8	Public Access, Local:	33
Phantom, Misc::	24		
Total:	168		168

Total Sightings: 168
Number of states reporting: 21
Most reports, State: CA (54)

Station Break,
Continued from page 3

hunters, that means more are coming.

2): Develop local knowledge of your area. This is an often overlooked principle—nothing takes the place of solid market information. This can help you zero in on probable miscue zones. It can be as simple as knowing what your local weather forecast is, and where the local stations broadcast from. (Note: Station mailing addresses and broadcast addresses are usually different. Invest some shoe leather in finding out where the towers are. This investment pays dividends.) Some TDers keep this information on maps.

As you get more advanced, learn the technical staff associated with your local live shows. Incompetent engineers, stage managers, and directors cause problems wherever they go. Back in 1979-80, for example, there was an engineer in the Bay Area, who will go nameless, that we followed first from show to show, and then from channel to channel (he was fired twice - imagine our joy when we would hear that he had been rehired by another unsuspecting channel), until he was finally bounced from our market altogether. The shows he was on invariably had problems, and by taping whatever show he was affiliated with, we enjoyed a huge hit rate. Though we lost track of him for a couple years, a friend sent a TD tape to us from San Bernardino in 1986, and lo and behold, there was the handiwork of Rodney Simpson (Oops, I promised not to tell.). He's long gone from S. B'dino, but keep your eyes out, he may be in your town by now.

Certain shows, too, have recurring problems. One here in S.F. is Channel 20's "Fifties Dance Party," show on Saturday mornings. Hardly a week goes by without a dancer kicking out a camera feed, or spinning poodle skirt first into the camera itself. As time goes by, this sort of knowledge will become second nature to you. But make a conscious effort now.

3): Educational channels. Most educational channels have students from local colleges working for them. More TD's occur here than in any other non-cable environment. Especially during the first couple weeks of any semester (and especially summer session!).

4): Start or join a local cult. There may be a Technical Diffi - Cult in your area. If not, start one. This makes the lonely job of monitoring less so. Take an area with 5 channels broadcasting 24 hours a day. If there are 20 members in your club, each of you can take responsibility for one six hour block a day (Remember, VCR's on Long Play can go for six hours per tape). That's means you've got everything covered in a sustainable fashion.

ȣ   ȣ   ȣ

Am told the smallest TV station in the country is KYUS, Channel 3 in Miles City, MT. The station manager and his wife are the programming execs, newscasters <u>and</u> the talk-show hosts. Any readers passing through that neck of the woods should check out the TD rate up there and report back. Sounds ripe.

ȣ   ȣ   ȣ

Thoughts on the new HDTV (High Definition Television) controversy. As most of you know, HDTV is supposedly the wave of the future. Introduced in Japan, it uses a different set of broadcast standards than the U.S.'s trusty NTSC guidelines. It supposedly provides for a clearer, sharper picture. This alone is bad enough. But HDTV will also destroy one of yours truly's favorite vacation pastimes. Europe and The U.S. are on different broadcast standards (those backward guys use PAL 625 line). HDTV threatens to standardize signal standards worldwide. This means the next time I am in France with my trusty Watchman, I'll be able to see the picture clearly, instead of with the cool melting effect I've got during my past two visits. I know some think that a switch to a new standard will mean plenty of TD's, and initially you are probably right. But that's only temporary. It represents another tightening of the seamless illusion of technological infallibility, and that's bad news. PSB recommends that you write your congressman (under the guise of a rational protectionist), and tell him to vote against HDTV.

ȣ   ȣ   ȣ

Coming By Summer: The Five Year Sighting Log: 1983-1988. It contains nearly 1,500 sightings of technical difficulties nationwide. Compiled by Sheila Duignan, Jim Morton and myself, with generous heapings of stuff from our loyal readers. Order forms in the next PSB.

ȣ   ȣ   ȣ

Quote: "Whatever is wrong in American life, you will find wrong in television."

-Herbert Brodkin
Producer, Playhouse 90

ȣ   ȣ   ȣ

Hope you get through your holidays without spilling your egg nog or some other technical difficulty. Until the spring issue (Late February), then, as always, KRRRRHHTZZZZZB!

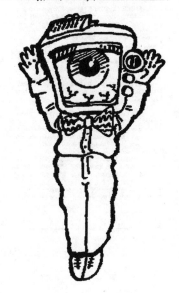

NEW TECHNICAL DIFFI-CULTS

BIG APPLE TOUGH TD'S, New York, NY: "Like The Jets & Giants, TD's are our goals."

A JOYFUL NOISE, Jackson, MS: Specializing in religious programming gaffes.

THE DIXIE PIXELS, Jackson, MS: "Catch a Buzz!"

TERRAPIN STATION, San Mateo, CA: Fans of both technical difficulties and The Grateful Dead. "Please Do Not Adjust Your Head."

THE RASTER-FARIANS, South San Francisco, CA: "Eternal Vigilance Is The Price Of Another TV."

PITCH & ROLL DIFFI-CULT & GIMLET SOCIETY, Spokane, WA.

ARKANSAS ERASER BACKS, University of Arkansas at Little Rock, AR: "Did You See What Arkansas?"

READER'S POLL RESULTS

FIVE MOST COMMON MUSICAL CHOICES FOR MUSIC PLAYED DURING BROADCAST INTERRUPTION (as reported by readers):

NUMBER	TITLE
1	"Don't Worry, Be Happy (instrumental)"
2	"Love Is Blue"
3	"Stand By Me"
4	"The Heat Is On"
5	"Brandenburg Concertos"

HOME TRADING CLUB

Twenty-five minutes (6 separate incidents) of rare SCROLLING VERTICAL BARS, 1981-88, from KIRO and KING, Seattle area. VHS only. Send have list for possible trades. PSB Box C9.

BOOM MIKE BLOOPERS. Assorted. Full two hour tape! VHS or BETA. To trade for cooking show glitches (grease fires, fallen souffles, etc.), especially from the 70's. PSB Box C10.

MONKEY ATTACK VIDEO! New! Live At Five broadcast from S.F. Zoo, where two monkeys attack reporter. All 90 seconds. To trade for high-quality (no later than second generation, please) Pit Bull-Los Angeles County Animal Control Office "bout" from April '87. "Spike," PSB Box B6.

MONDAY NIGHT FOOTBALL'S FAMOUS FINGER BROADCAST, to trade for your local public access channel nonsense. PSB Box C11.

Have three years of CHILLY BILLY SATURDAY NIGHT MONSTER MOVIE glitches (WTAE, Ch 4, Pittsburgh). Was the host of Creature Features an alcoholic? Why was he always dropping his mystic chalice, and causing his dungeon set to topple over? Was it for frightening effect that he slurred his speech? And who was asleep at the switch when he or his midget servant, Drachma, would let out another filthy epithet? Good enough to keep me awake til 3:00 AM every Saturday from 1982-84. Must see. Choice. "Warlord," PSB Box C12.

WANTED: Who's willing to part with a copy of Guy Lombardo, Junior's lone attempt at hosting a New Year's Eve

WANTED: '72 WMAQ F—K You Charlie bulletin. Will trade anything in my collection: Faces of Death II, amateur smut (quality bad). Have some World Series uncensored feeds, can get Lords stuff. RSVP ASAP: PSB C14

WANTED: WMAQ F— U Charley Special Report bulletin. Prefer to trade but will pay cash. Send your want list. PSB C15

Nudes! Listing of ALL nude scenes in 1300 R–rated films; listed by running time (hour/min/sec). Program your VCR to record only the GOOD STUFF on late–nite cable! $29.95 money order only (postage paid). "The Krugmeister," PSB B3.

Lonely TD collector seeks female companion. Age unimportant. Must love sci–fi and TD collecting. No alcohol or smoking. Mel Shepard, PSB C16. No calls.

Spittin' Kitten tributes! Bodily fluids reclassified/animated. The hollow rattle of brass casings hitting the concrete forces the viewer to contemplate the velocity/tonnage of impending cleavage. The OBVIOUS! 16 millimeter trailers from HADES! Celluloid atrocities purloined and CORRECTED. With Traci, Maryam, Pam, Zoë, Eileen, Kimberly, Luciana, and many more. The OBVIOUS: 30–minute videotape. Will trade for anything that interests me. Speak. Peter Flechette, 433 Kearny, Suite 433, San Francisco CA 94108.

COMPUTATION OF QUEST QUOTIENT

$$QQ = \frac{(M_d/100 + M_f/1000 + P/10 + L/5 + (I \times 10) + D + T) \times DA}{(F/10) + (\$/100) + 1}$$

Mileage driven: $M_d = 0$
Mileage flown: $M_f = 0$
Phone calls: $P = 32$
Letters: $L = 6$
Intimacies: $I = 0$
Drop Dead factor: $D = 2$
Days spent: $T = 5$

Difficulty-Aggravation multiplier: $DA = 2$

Failure rate: $F = 0$
Cost: $\$ = 100$

QUEST QUOTIENT = 11.4

☞ *Analysis:*

Hard to gauge Aggravation factor since much of the work was performed by Mike-Ian. He seems to have had a pretty good time, though. . . . Because Harper's came to me, Actual Difficulty (as opposed to Anticipated Difficulty) factor registered first 0 in American Quest history! . . . Number of upset people is conservative assessment, counting only Lapham and KDIO station manager.

"USHER, STOP THE MOVIE: I DROPPED A PENNY!"

FRIGHT NIGHT 2
1245 300 515
730 945

NO PASSES BATMAN
1145 130
230 415
515 700
945 800
1045

ADULT $600
CHILDREN
UNDER 12 $350
BARGAIN
PRICE $350

BEVERAGES POPCORN

$2.50 $2.00 $1.75 $3.50 $2.75 $2.00

TAX INCLUDED   TAX INCLUDED

Life in a Multiplex

et us in! Let us in!" The mob harmon-ically surges, like ebony waves lapping silkily on the beach of an oil-slicked bay, toward the velvet ropes, then recedes, sending those on the periphery stumbling toward the candy

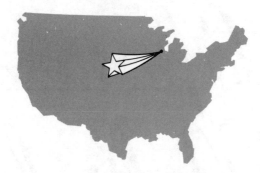

counter, the exit doors, or Theaters 5 and 6, where last week's passions, *Indiana Jones* and *Ghostbusters 2*, echo through empty halls. Rather than queue outside on this balmy summer evening, the id-propelled swarm has elected to infest the lobby, where, like members of the Locusts Union on payday, they threaten to strip clean the stock of the candy counter. And now the music, the roaring sound effects, the snatches of dialogue caught through the crack between the doors —it has driven them into a frenzy. The ten o'clock show of *Batman* in Theaters 7 and 8 has over an hour yet to unspool, but the midnight crowd wants in—*now*.

The theater manager, known as Miss L, who had admitted ticket holders early to boost concession sales, confronts the mob with steely resolve. The swaying of the ropes causes the mighty stanchions to rock, and as Miss L moves to steady the barrier, she slips.

Instantly the crowd is upon her. They threaten to devour Miss L and storm what one wag—guess who?—calls "the Bat-stille." Four ushers rush into the fray, terrified but energized. Local TV crews, on hand to cover the spectacle of the summer's hottest movie premiering at the city's largest multiplex, are getting more than they bargained for. These aren't harmless (okay, *pathetic*) nerds in Joker-face, this is a reign of terror, kicked off by a simple "Let them eat popcorn!"

The ushers and Miss L, back on her feet, repel the mob, but there is no Jimmy Stewart here to shame the rabble and bring them to their senses. The cavalrylike appearance of twelve cops, however, does have the desired effect. Order is restored, and typical, everyday beastliness resumes.

There is a perception that moviegoing isn't what it used to be, that the excitement once felt when the lights dimmed and the curtains parted is diminished in labyrinthine multiplexes with fake butter and high prices. Megachains like Canadian-based Cineplex Odeon are promising to restore "that great movie feeling" by building new facilities with state-of-the-art stuff and everything. (These boasts are usually issued contemporaneously with announcements of new, state-of-the-art pricing policies.) But after scientifically investigating the moviegoing experience by rolling up the sleeves of my lab coat and working in the trenches at Chicagoland's Norridge Theaters—a perfectly ordinary tenplex serving a paradigm of Middle America—on *Batman*'s opening weekend, I have found that it is not the physical plant of the movie theater that has become so wretched, it is the audience. Moviegoers are—and maybe always have been, but we'll never know for sure because no questing social scientist in the past ever conducted such an investigation—scum.

I'm not talking about fatuous chatterboxes calling the onscreen play-by-play or conducting braying kaffeeklatsches; I'm talking Dixie cups of brown goo and knife fights in the parking lot and fungus-y bare feet in your hair and beer-can tributes launched at the screen, grenade-style. I'm talking about a typical weekend at a typical multiplex. This is my quest.

☞ T h u r s d a y

The Old Orchard theater, in Skokie, Illinois, is, for me, the closest thing to a hometown Bijou. Unfortunately, this classy fourplex figures to be nice and clean and safe and quiet—*Batman* isn't even opening here. However, it is the only place at which I have been able to get permission to work. I pestered several chains—including Cineplex Odeon, which runs many, many, many theaters in Chicagoland and elsewhere but is as congenial to journalists as are Skokians to neo-Nazis—but only Loews (owned, incidentally, by my pals, the Coca-Cola Company), which recently ate up M&R, which owned the Old Orchard, will allow me the access I need to perform my quest, and this is where they have placed me.

Time for a figurative footnote about Cineplex Odeon (known as Cineplex Odious to those who call it that), the industry's pacesetter —when it comes to hiking ticket prices, supplanting "trailers" for upcoming movies with "goddamn TV commercials," and charging for extra butter. Among their other popular features: ushers who open up the exterior doors during matinees, letting daylight come streaming in; more ushers who walk up and down the aisles all through the movie, shining a flashlight on people who put their feet on the seats —except at the Times Square showings of *Do the Right Thing*; and concessions prices that don't include tax, as if the profit margin on a two-dollar Coke isn't enough to absorb the extra sixteen cents.

Cineplex owns the Woodside Theater in Schaumburg, Illinois, which is truly the perfect locale for this quest, being appended to one of America's first and greatest modern-style shopping malls. My primary mistake was in contacting the local office: nobody who works for an overbearing company like this will ever accept responsibility at the local level. I contacted Patricia Wexler in Chicago, who asked me how much I was planning to pay them for this; my initial reaction was, Great—a sense of humor! Wrong.

Wexler, not knowing me very well, thought she could wriggle off the hook gracefully: "I checked with the legal department, and much as I'm sure they could use the extra help [yuk-yuk, slurp-slurp], it's against company policy for nonemployees to work at the theater. Okay?" I threatened to go and apply for a job like a civilian; she didn't seem too worried.

With my growing realization that I was not actually "working" during my quests per se, but, rather, *observing*, I re-approached her, abandoning all pretense of becoming a temporary employee and thus avoiding her excuse. Eluding the sack, Wexler rolled out, then handed off: "I asked corporate headquarters, and we felt that with the summer and all, we'll take a pass."

Again, the implication is that they really appreciate my "interest," but I'm obviously confusing them with a corporation that gives a shit. I tried to get this in writing from Lynda Friendly, Cineplex's intimidating corporate spin doctor in Toronto, but never received a reply. Big surprise.

My first day at the Old Orchard is daunting; as I feared, this theater is far from typical. The audience is affluent and mature, and the theater is clean and spiffy, with large screens and comfy seats. I ask the ushers for wacky stories. "There's this guy we call the Phantom Masturbator," says one, and the others nod excitedly. "He likes Theater Four. He always sits near a woman. Once we chased him out to the parking lot and got his license number."

"What movies does he like?"

"Last time it was during *Scandal* [starring Bridget Fonda (!)], and another time it was, let's see . . . *Moonstruck!*"

The head usher, Michael Samaniego, sixteen, asks if I'd like to visit the booth. My impression of projectionists is that, belonging to a strong union, they are generally paranoid about anybody invading their workplace. But Michael assures me the projectionist is his pal; he takes pride in the total coolness of his friendship with a grownup who represents a sort of tattoos-and-nudie-calendar union toughness. Ascending the stairs, he ticks off his duties: checking the toilet paper, the exits, and the air conditioning, setting up the poles, and keeping track of the other ushers. We enter the booth; the projectionist studies me quickly, then shrugs. "Okay, take a look . . . *and scram.*"

I'll hang out with the ushers. Even at the nicey-nice Old Orchard, I learn, delinquents of all ages sneak in constantly. When caught, none ever challenges the usher, who is backed by a combat-hungry pack of co-workers. The ushers love to swoop down on rogues, especially little-kid rogues; it makes their day.

I ask about perks. "Free movies," I am told amid snorts of disgust. After Loews bought out M&R, a policy of complimentary soda and popcorn for employees was discontinued, as were Christmas bonuses, which averaged twenty dollars or so. As per Loews policy, ushers wear black pants, black shoes, black socks, a black bowtie, a white shirt, a maroon jacket, and a name tag. The floor manager, who ranks above the head ushers but below the assistant managers, sports a frilly tuxedo shirt.

What about cantankerous patrons? I am told "the customer is always right": a moviegoer can receive a refund as late as *forty-five minutes* into a film for even the most harebrained of reasons. Complaints include "offensive subject matter" or rambunctious neighbors ("Why didn't I move? Why should *I* move?"), but even "the film is boring" will work. The manager will offer a ticket to another film in the multiplex. I am told of reptilian cranks who will "do" every film in the multiplex in an hour, raising their arms in disgust and loudly searching for the manager after giving each film about ten minutes.

This leads to the popular question, Can I pay just one admission and spend an entire day at the multiplex seeing every film? The answer is equivocally yes—as long as your conscience will allow you to *steal* and *trespass*. At most multiplexes, security is pretty lax about crossing from one theater to another, especially if you switch in the middle of a film. You can go to the bathroom and return to a different theater, or just boldly stride from one theater to another; few ushers would follow and disrupt an entire audience.

Batmania escalates. On the radio I hear a news item: the owner of Chicago's 400 Twin Theater wants to jump out of a helicopter in a Batman suit, but Warner Brothers and DC Comics have slapped an injunction preventing this great fun, claiming copyright infringement.

☞ Friday

I *must* switch to a theater showing *Batman*. I beseech M&R, and am shifted to the Norridge, a tenplex presenting *Batman* on three screens. (Emotional bonus: Norridge Park was the home of *AmQuest* back-cover artist John Wayne Gacy—his now-demolished pad was not far from the theater.) I zoom over for the first show.

I hook up with Dennis Chance, seventeen, a "sort-of-head usher." He's been here a mere three months, but, as he cockily asserts, "I've, y'know, *got it*." And he has, strutting with authority and performing his duties as second nature. He, too, is "tight" with the projectionist and eagerly leads me up to the booth. Here I am shown a process called "interlock," which in the filmmaking world refers to unwed picture and sound being projected in sync, but in exhibition refers to a single print of a film being shown almost simultaneously in two different theaters.

The print rests horizontally in one piece on a huge rotating platter. It spools through projector A, appears on screen A, and flutters across the booth through a jerry-built system of pulleys and supports, snaking around corners and bypassing obstructions, where it is fed through projector B and seen, seconds after appearing on screen A, on screen B. (Ushers like to "freak out" by darting from theater A to B and catching the same scene twice.) Then, if all goes well, the print returns along the same route to projector A's takeup platter. When a print breaks in normal projection it creates a tangle of celluloid and incites stomping and whistling; when it snaps during interlock, the film goes whirring into the vast recesses of the projection booth, and incites *stereo* stomping and whistling. A film in interlock must be constantly monitored for sags in the pathway; projectionists *love* it. That was sarcasm.

Previews start promptly at showtime. House lights remain on until the feature begins. (If we were within Chicago city limits, I am told, an ordinance would dictate that house lights be left on during the show so that one might see the perverts.) It's been a grand tour, but once again the projectionists are getting *that great union feeling* and

I am telepathically nudged toward the doorway. We have to be going anyway, for it's almost between-show time, and as Dennis explains, "The head usher has to spend a lot of time looking for the other ushers."

I meet the pleasant, earnest Eric, known as Zulu, who is on the cleanup crew but hopes to become an usher. He skates through the soda-slicked theater between shows scooping up popcorn buckets, cups, and a repulsive array of things so foul that even trashy people have chosen to discard them. "So, Zulu, what's the weirdest thing you've found under a seat?" He smiles, replying, "A pair of black lace panties, a wet condom, a used tampon. . . . " And he'd rather *tear tickets?* Today is Zulu's day off, but he's helping to clean up anyway—!! As it is for many here, this theater is his social life; after all, they spend every Friday and Saturday night here, and on days off come to see free movies. In fact, Zulu met his girlfriend, a former candy-counter staffer, here.

Raging hormones ping and carom like popcorn in a popper; the bulk of the crew are high-schoolers feeling the first cramps of lust. Ushers have their brainwaves tuned to "Music to Watch Girls By," while concession-stand cuties make suggestive remarks and pass notes to the boys. Interemployee dating is Topic A when the crew goes on break; the only non–Dating Game exchange I heard all weekend was when ushers and concessionettes tried to piece together the plot of *Batman* from moments they had been able to snatch here and there.

The average multiplex is far too understaffed to post an usher inside the theater, extending an opportunity for lo-cost moviegoing: one member of a group buys a ticket, then admits his pals through an interior exit door after the show starts. Caveat 1: During daylight, the piercing rays from outdoors are a dead giveaway; you'd be surprised, the ushers assure me, just how many do-gooder civilians will turn you in. Caveat 2: The Beave tried to do this on an episode of "Leave It to Beaver," and he got caught.

There's a commotion up front. A headstrong usher, Ray, has impulsively retired and is antsily pacing, awaiting his final paycheck. "I couldn't take all the bullshit," he explains. What happened was, nobody remembered to change the sign under the *Batman* poster in the lobby from COMING SOON to NOW PLAYING. Ray was taking tickets. "A guy with a *Batman* ticket sees the sign and asks me—he's got a ticket, and it's only playing in *three theaters* here—'Isn't *Batman* open yet?' So I said, 'No, it'll be here in a few weeks.' And I got chewed out for that."

☞ Saturday

When I punch in before the 11:45 A.M. show, there is a line; it started at seven this morning. The first show on weekends is the discount show, and these people are going to get that discount, goddammit. *Batman* has been shifted to larger quarters, with the depopularized *Ghostbusters* retreating. After the hysteria of a sold-out bargain show, the lobby clears out, the box office takes a breather— it's a beautiful day, and the rest of the matinees figure to be about half full—and out come the brooms.

As I sweep popcorn and wrappers into the dustpan, I think wistfully of the grand old movie palaces: ushers wore snappy, color-coordinated uniforms with shiny buttons and jaunty hats; they wielded their flashlights like a maestro his baton; they tore tickets with white-glove aplomb; they suavely seated Cary Grant–ish patrons; they delivered babies, got discovered by Hollywood producers, and had an elan, a polish, that befitted their glamour profession. They were cool. Nowadays: sweep, sweep, sweep.

I hang out with Darek Rembowski, who's been here a week but seems to have the rhythm (as well as a new admirer, the flirtatious candy girl Andie). These days, he tells me, with school out and crowds so big and a teenage work force that scoffs at minimum wage, ushers are putting in seventy-hour weeks. With midnight shows on Fridays and Saturdays and morning shows on weekends, the weary crew goes home for two or three hours' sleep and then returns—Zulu, who swept up after the midnight show until well past 3 A.M., slept on a couch-bed in the office last night.

The ushers' Il Duce is floor manager Eustacchio Giuliani, a junior at Triton College who plans to be a dentist. "Stosh," who has been here four and a half years and is built like a granite tombstone, is an ideal conduit between management, who would like things to run smoothly, labor, who want to have fun and meet girls (or boys), and the public, who want to behave like this is one of those dreams where you know you're dreaming so you can do or say anything you want because after all it's only a dream.

Psychologically, the most intimidating job is "working the rope," that is, facing down the mob so they won't storm into the theater before the previous show ends and one's fellow ushers have had a chance to clean up. The crowd desperately wants that rope to come down; any false move, any unexpected noise, can cause a stampede.

Kevin Leineweber, twenty, a junior at Indiana (*Breaking Away*) University, a personable head usher, helps me work the rope. "I see everything different since I've been working here," he says. "This [nodding at mob in lobby] is my barnyard. These [indicating theaters] are my holding pens. And there [pointing to concession stand] is the trough."

Through the open doors of the theater, we see a *Peter Pan* trailer unspooling. A lardy, food-laden beardo pushes past us, beholds the chirping cartoon characters onscreen and whinily frets that *Batman* has started. A child runs up to Kevin: somebody's throwing food. Although nobody confesses or identifies the malefactor, Kevin's head-usher instincts pinpoint the culprit, based on the item thrown, its trajectory, and the way people look.

After the show, I help clean up the yecch left by the finest people in the world, our customers. It's more like triage: you do the best you can, trying to make every seat habitable and less of a rat buffet. One usher spots a ten-dollar bill, which must be split with the other four ushers (anything five dollars or over is shared). Found money is an appropriate dividend, considered a "tip." Ushers can average ten or twenty dollars a week in these gratuities—almost enough to pay for the shoes and clothes ruined by the appalling goo discarded by our valued patrons.

It's Saturday night, and Windy City cinéastes are arrhythmically pounding at the glass doors. The amazing Stosh is in overdrive; he repeatedly discovers last-minute seats, even doubles. Each time he does—kachinggg!—Warner Brothers earns six dollars. Loews' regional manager, Jerry Kerley, is on the premises and checking things out, but few are concerned; at worst they might get chewed out (he complains that ushers don't "walk the theater," that is, saunter brassily down the aisles at intervals during the show to demonstrate the presence of authority), but with everyone quitting, their jobs are safe. The din is punctuated by shrieks from the candy counter as those overheated, vixenish candy gals drop ice down one another's backs.

Outside, the crowd on line is periodically cheering "Yayyy!" or "Ooooh!" A street magician delighting a captive audience? No, they are watching breathlessly as passersby obliviously promenade past a fresh heap of vomit: "Ooooh!" if they miss it, "Yayyy!" if they don't.

Pat, the assistant manager, fetches the "Puke Stuff," a powder that absorbs semiliquids so that an usher with a broom can sweep them up. Of course, the usher has to do it in front of the rabid, nasty crowd. Not too cool for scouting chicks.

"You know how when you've worked as a waiter you leave better tips when you go out?" I say rhetorically to my fellow theater cleaners, knee-deep in unspeakable rubbish. "Well, when you guys go to other theaters do you carry your garbage out to the trash cans?"

They pause, look at each other, and sneer, as if I were a Dixie cup of brown goo. "Hell, no," says one. "We do to *them* what they do to *us*." The others nod emphatically.

☞ S u n d a y

Last night, a guy working the candy counter dropped a supersize Coke onto the already slick floor, then did a pratfall, landing on his coccyx (that's his tailbone). A thousand patrons, Gosh love 'em, cheered lustily. He was mortified, but that's show biz. Now it's my turn.

Several staffers have called in "sick"—the maroon flu. Even though I have spent three days making notes and roving while ostensibly "working" here, today they can actually use my help; I pour sodas for a monotonous few hours, and the staff begins treating me like one of their own—except that I hate their disposable music and tomorrow I will be gone (whereas they might hang on another week). I learn how to spew golden flavor onto popcorn: three, five, or seven squirts, depending on bucket size. The kernels are popped in yummy coconut oil; butter-hued salt is sprinkled on for "golden color."

Usher Jim Giambalvo, seventeen, tells me how much he enjoys interacting with "people," and shows me a pocketful of slips with girls' phone numbers to prove it. Another usher returns from break, entering the theater through handleless doors with the secret usher's technique. A few bratty kids observe and absorb, figurative lightbulbs shining above their heads.

"The best time of all," Stosh says, "is when we see kids sneaking in. We let them sit down, we watch them, then, when they go to the candy counter, we let them buy armsful of food—they're so loaded down they can hardly move. Then, when they try to go back into the theater, we throw them out with all that stuff."

The line is building for the next show. Stosh, ever the prankster, orders an excitable young usher, Victor, to go through the line and politely say to everyone, "Thank you for coming to M&R/Loews Theaters." "Oh, no," says Victor, "they'll laugh at me." "You gotta do it," says Stosh. Victor begins at the back of the line; patrons are tremendously amused. Stosh and I watch from inside; we cannot hear, but we see Victor, red-faced, gamely making his way through the line. Those he has greeted are convulsed with laughter, gleefully pointing out Victor to those who missed his speech. Soon the whole line is chortling at this zygote of courtesy amidst such anarchy. And it's pretty funny, actually.

★ ★ ★ ★ ★ ★ ★ ★ ★ ★ ★ ★ ★ ★ ★ ★ ★ ★ ★

Usher's Ranking of Jobs

FROM WORST TO NOT THE WORST

1) Polishing stanchions (busy work for slack times). It's nasty work.
2) Ticket taking. Boring; usually a two-hour shift, and you can't move around and flirt.
3) Checking women's washroom. Potentially embarrassing.
4) Cleaning out theater. Gross, but you find money.
5) Sweeping lobby. Demeaning, but you can talk to the girls at the candy counter.

WHAT THEY LIKE TO DO

1) Seating "people" (girls).

COMPUTATION OF QUEST QUOTIENT

$$QQ = \frac{(M_d/100 + M_f/1000 + P/10 + L/5 + (I \times 10) + D + T) \times DA}{(F/10) + (\$/100) + 1}$$

Mileage driven: $M_d = 150$
Mileage flown: $M_f = 1900$
Phone calls: $P = 21$
Letters: $L = 6$
Intimacies: $I = 0$
Drop Dead factor: $D = 2$
Days spent: $T = 4$

Difficulty-Aggravation multiplier: $DA = 9$

Failure rate: $F = 0$
Cost: $\$ = 500$

QUEST QUOTIENT = 19.0

☞ *Analysis:*

Whew, what a DA factor—one more mind-blowing round of fruitless "negotiation" with Cineplex Odeon would have made this a 10! . . . Add that to a job I wouldn't do again for all the p's in Piccolapuppilla, and you've got a big number 9, mister. . . . Overheard at matinee: FIVE- *(as in* Easy Pieces*)* YEAR-OLD: *"Oh, man—Nicholson!"*

Pogo the Clown

John Wayne Gacy has been called the Killer Clown: a man who used to slap on greasepaint and dress up as a wacky character he called Pogo to cheer sick children—and who also is credited with torturing and murdering, by strangulation, thirty-three teenage Chicagoans and burying them under his house. He is now the most industrious man on death row, a prisoner who has adjusted to confinement in a seven-by-eight-foot cell so well that he has forged a thriving career as a painter—his most popular subject being himself as Pogo—while his fellow inmates piddle away their days watching soap operas and flipping playing cards into hats.

When I first acquired one of his Pogo paintings as a Christmas gift, I knew this work had to adorn the cover of this book. Pogo is a symbol of my America: a cheery exterior that warbles "Don't Worry, Be Happy," but a sinister interior that hums "Back Stabbers."

Gacy possesses a very positive, very American trait—one that he horribly misapplied, true, yet a virtue that stood him in good stead in his community prior to the discovery of his foul deeds: he was a relentlessly hard worker. (His two favorite painters are Michelangelo and Leonardo da Vinci; both, he says, were workaholics, like himself.) Gacy was no common killer; he was as suited to prodigious homicide as surely as his heroes (and frequent subjects) Emmett Kelly and Don Quixote were to professional clowning and delusionary windmill tilting, respectively. According to newspaper reports, as well as Tim Cahill's *Buried Dreams* and Clifford Linedecker's *The Man Who Killed Boys*, Gacy put all his considerable assets—carpentry skills, physical strength, persuasiveness, indefatigability, status in the community, intimidation factor of being an employer of unskilled teens—into doing what he was doing. You or I could never kill thirty-three boys, one at a time, without getting caught. That's why he's in *Guinness* and we're not.

In addition to the beguiling Pogo, I feel another connection to Gacy: we were both born in the same Chicago hospital, Edgewater. In the mid-1970s, while Gacy was rampaging throughout the North Side, I was bar-hopping and cruising the same neighborhoods. Had I been looking for work, it could have been me contributing to the sickening stench pervading his house on Summerdale Avenue.

Anyway, I want to use the Pogo painting on the cover of *American Quest*. There will be two hurdles: my publisher and Gacy himself. I don't know how either is going to respond.

Unexpectedly, the publisher is a pushover. Sure I can use Pogo; the only restriction is that it cannot be the sole image on the cover. (The tune changes, however, as the publication date approaches. Sales reps don't like the perception—faulty or not—that their products glorify mass murderers. Pogo is shunted to the back cover and shrunk. I could say more, but . . .)

A bigger surprise comes when I write to Gacy and receive the promptest, most courteous and helpful response I will receive from anybody all year. Knowing that he is a "can-do" guy, as opposed to the "might-do, if you make it worth my while" types I have been dealing with, this should not have surprised me.

In an early letter he tells me to address him not as "Mr. Gacy," but as "John" or "J.W.," stating he is not "a formal-type person." Contrast this with Richard Nunis, the president of Disney World, who is so formal he never even responds to a fretful father's letter. J.W. also encloses an attractive listing of his available paintings. (You can get a copy by writing him at N00921, Lock Box 711, Menard, IL 62259. Prices are very reasonable.) This civility from a man who undoubtedly receives some of the scariest, nastiest hate mail imaginable. At Christmas, I become one of one hundred and fifty Gacy correspondents to receive an attractive handmade Christmas card. At Christmas, from Dennis Hopper and Peter Fonda—*bupkis.*

Soon I find myself formulating an opinion on the death penalty, something that never really bothered me much before. I read accounts of remorseless Louisiana death row mad dogs who stab pregnant mothers of ten for bus fare—and I believe it is wrong to lump J.W. with them. John is making a contribution to our culture with his art; while he should clearly never be allowed to buy a bag of Sakrete again, it would be wrong to execute somebody who has something positive to offer.

I know there will be people teed off at me for "aggrandizing a mass murderer," but really, all I am doing is reproducing a clown painting that I like. It's true that the work has extra resonance— okay, a lot—because of its artist's infamy, but that's what makes it the perfect face of *American Quest.* If necessary, I could justify this as a commentary on celebrity in our culture, point out that our society shows more respect for a man who grabs headlines even through a heinous act than for "real" artists. And who's to say, maybe that *is* what this is all about. (Do the people who buy Tony Curtis paintings have to go through all this rationalization?)

In a *New York Times* story about a show of J.W.'s work in Boston, a huffy "artist" grumbles that "Gacy is living an artist's dream. . . . He has all the time to enjoy painting that he wants without worrying about paying the rent. . . . I think that's despicable." An artist's dream? I am sure that J.W. would switch places with this guy in a second—except that then he'd lose all that extra resonance, and probably a healthy measure of his talent.

After about a dozen promptly written, mutually cordial letters (Gacy has pen pals all over the world—in fact, a book of his correspondence has been published), I falter and do not respond to a letter. (I was on the road with my Kissy quest.) A few weeks later, Gacy writes that he is feeling suspicions of betrayal and abuse on my part. What gripes him most is that I had earlier told him how much I despised people who ignored my letters while doing *American Quest*, and here, he cannily points out, I am doing just that to him. He's right, of course.

I can appreciate his feeling of helplessness: he is confined and unable to keep track of what people are writing and saying about him. No doubt he has been exploited by the press in the past; stories sympathetic to convicted mass murderers are not exactly a staple of journalism. I must admit, however, that the idea of John Wayne Gacy being pissed off at me is more than a bit unsettling. It adds an unexpected and undesired dimension of potential reality to the Drop Dead factor.

COMPUTATION OF QUEST QUOTIENT

$$QQ = \frac{(M_d/100 + M_f/1000 + P/10 + L/5 + (I \times 10) + D + T) \times DA}{(F/10) + (\$/100) + 1}$$

Mileage driven: $M_d = 0$
Mileage flown: $M_f = 0$
Phone calls: $P = 8$
Letters: $L = 9$
Intimacies: $I = 0$
Drop Dead factor: $D = 66$
Days spent: $T = 0$

Difficulty-Aggravation multiplier: $DA = 1$

Failure rate: $F = 50$
Cost: $\$ = 280$

QUEST QUOTIENT = 7.8

☞ *A n a l y s i s :*

Drop Dead factor is what this one's all about. Number is conservatively computed as parents of J.W.'s victims (33 times 2). And who can blame them? But surely there will be more who will not like this—envious "artists" and do-nothing intellectuals who know what "semiotics" means, for example—but that number can only be computed after publication. . . . DA of 1 reflects fact that, despite fears that no publisher would allow J.W.'s artwork on a book cover, and that artist himself might not agree to this, J.W. was easily most cooperative and efficient person with whom I dealt in year of American Quest. It's only the truth. . . . Failure rate (F) of 50% reflects Pogo's demotion to back cover.

South of the Border

If (damaged) memory serves, Carlos Casta-neda, the mystical "literary" guru of '70s pothead colle-gians, posited that there is a unique spot on earth for each of us, a sacred site, from which we can draw untold reservoirs

of energy, making us omnipotent, or at least "all that we can be." The trick is to find that spot. Some successful people, for whom there can be no other explanation, clearly have found their power spots: "Weird Al" Yankovic, George Steinbrenner, Joe Piscopo, Geraldo Rivera, Madonna. My spiritual pal Roy wonders what would happen if he were to discover *his* spot beneath a conveyor belt on a moving assembly line at the Ford Motors plant in Dearborn, Michigan; he could claim the spot, jogging to stay in place, and, because he would be so powerful, nobody would be able to dislodge him. But if they shut down the line without his noticing, he would jog off his spot, and they could then pound him senseless.

I bring this up because there is one place—right here in America, of course—that makes me feel really topnotch every time I'm there. It may not be a "power spot," but then this isn't the '70s, either, although I hear that Disco Tex and his Sex-o-lettes are making a comeback. It's a place that never fails to make me feel—as Andy Griffith used to describe the taste of different stuff smeared on a Ritz cracker—uhhmmm, uhhmmm . . . goo-oo-oood, *goood*. South of the Border, South Carolina, seems designed to nurture the inner me: lots of buildings open twenty-four hours, postcard racks aplenty, nice warm neon, big, colorful plaster animal statues, and an adjacent su-perhighway humming me soothingly into a beta state.

South of the Border is well known to all who have traveled the Eastern seaboard via I-95; its wacky billboards beckon for 400 miles, from Virginia to Georgia. Known as SOB, the place is America's grandest roadside stop, a bright, neon-lit, Mexican-themed (circa Frito Bandito) village that includes 14 shops, 6 restaurants, a 290-room motel, a 100-site campground, a 9-hole golf course, a convention center–bingo emporium, a burgeoning amusement park, and two of America's most successful fireworks stores, Lo-Bo's and Fort Pedro.

If the billboards aren't enough, the 135-acre complex, which beckons irresistibly from the interstate (a study showed that one in three out-of-state cars stops here), is heralded by: an enormous new computer-controlled electric sign comprising 24,576 incandescent bulbs; the 220-foot Sombrero Tower; and a 104-foot, 77-ton rendition of a jolly Mexican fellow—SOB's mascot, Pedro.

SOB is more, however, than the gaudy epitome of roadside hyperbole—there is a "there" there. Founder and sole owner Alan Schafer began this place forty years ago with a vision of profits and self-amusement; that vision has evolved into the most entertaining pit stop along any highway in the country, and therefore on earth. In the past four decades, under Schafer's unorthodox stewardship, SOB has gone from being a convenient halfway point for Florida vacations to a primary destination in and of itself.

So when July 4 rolled around, I asked myself where I'd most like to be. Let's see, July 4 means:

➢ Lots of travelers . . .
➢ Getting drunker and louder and hornier and stupider . . .
➢ And "celebrating" with . . .
➢ Fireworks.

July 4 means . . . SOB! Fort Pedro and Lo-Bo's are just over the border from North Carolina, where fireworks sales are illegal. There will be swarms of restless crackers crammed onto minimal acreage with an urge to splurge and nowhere else to go—SOB is a Fantasy Island amidst a sea of Mayberrys, RFD. This should make for a rowdy, sultry, fireworked-up, Carolina-in-July melting pot—the kind of atmosphere that normally sends me scrambling for air-conditioned cover. What would happen, I conjectured, if I subjected myself to this boisterous siege by signing on as an SOB staffer for the holiday weekend? Will Jane and Johnny Reb shell-shock my mind into salsaed grits? Can Pedro's magic withstand this severest test of all?

☞ Saturday

I drove all day Friday and arrived here last night. Dusk comes after 9 P.M. this time of year, and the prolonged "magic hour"—the Sombrero Tower, green and red lights glowing brighter by the minute, assuming its full powers of scenic dominance; the electric sign surging with energy; the sky glowing orange, the atmosphere tingling with fading rays from nature's horizon and throbbing with the pulsating neon of man; the streaming headlights of travelers seeking caravansary—never seemed more fantastical. The bewitching aura, tempered by the ever-present menace of lurching, overheated autos attacking from every point of my personal compass, made me want to walk to "it," like the spaceship in *Close Encounters*. But I couldn't, because I was already inside "it." All I could do was let it permeate my soul. . . .

I arise early. I think I have recovered from last night's "magic hour." Hoo-boy, that sure was mesmerizing—I seem to recall waxing weird. Fortunately, a group of helpful little moppets slammed cherry bombs to the pavement all night long in an effort to "deprogram" the motel's overnight guests. Carolyn, SOB's director of public relations, fetches me in a golf cart for an overview of the grounds. For those of you who haven't cruised around in a golf cart for a while but remember it being kind of fun, I have a news flash—it's, like, wow. If the most loathsome boss on earth, say Leona Helmsley, called tomorrow and offered me a minimum-wage job inspecting maggoty hog carcasses *while cruising around in a golf cart*, I would merrily accept.

We zip behind the scenes, exposing me to the Pedros behind the Pedro: SOB has its own water-and-sewer, landscaping, laundry, electrical, police, fire, and sanitation departments. The nearest town, Dillon, is ten minutes away, so SOB—the largest employer in the county—has by necessity become a self-sufficient little city. The SOB fire department mainly combats electrical fires—although one time a big army truck from Fort Bragg took out a gas pump and caused some tense, inflammable moments for the volunteer crew. I keep an eye peeled for explosives-bearing young miscreants; they manage to evade my radar.

We pass an authentic-looking barrio-style mural behind the Myrtle Beach Shop. Carolyn tells me it was commissioned from an artist last year. I am disquieted by its reality: after all, the image of Pedro is just an advertising hook, a springboard for humor, and has about as much to do with real-life Chicanos as Charlie Chaplin's Little Tramp had to do with actual freezing, grimy, not-getting-the-cute-blind-girl-in-the-end homeless persons. (While Schafer is certainly tuned-in enough to know that one has to watch oneself when characterizing *any* racial group, he has thankfully not backed down too much through the past few decades of "sensitivity," and SOB proudly retains its zany pseudo-Mexicality in an age when the "least offensive programming" theory has invaded all aspects of life. Schafer did, however, discontinue a curious billboard that trumpeted the pro-rape slogan, "When it's inevitable, relax and enjoy it.")

Carolyn escorts me into the truckers' store, an area that is off-limits to nontruckers and thus as enticing to me as a girls' bathroom. The magazine rack alone, which I assume must be groaning under unimaginably abstruse pornography with titles like *Stumpy Misses* or *Lesbo First Ladies*, will certainly provide more stimulation than even a film adaptation of the Victoria's Secret catalogue. But *US* and *People* have displaced this grand old tradition. Boo-hoo: sometimes I *do* identify with Charles Kuralt. In the back of the store is a well-appointed lounge, with TV and a quiet bank of phones.

One commodity in short supply—to nontruckers—at SOB is a quiet place to make a phone call. One phone is located in the parking lot of the convenience store, where callers must endure a steady litany of vociferous shouts from the cabs of four-by-fours clarifying beer preferences, along with the revving of unmuffled Confederate engines. Another phone, the one I choose, is in the vestibule of the gift shop, adjacent to a witless byproduct of the computer-chip revolution—a twenty-five-cent "amusement" machine that is capable of verbally grabbing the attention of passersby. And, oh, if only my pickup patter were as smooth as that of the distortedly overamplified, electronically simulated Brooklynese voice: "Hey, where ya' goin'? Hey—what's yer name? Hey!" Note to Silicon Valley—work on that smoochy sound that women love to hear.

We encounter Schafer, who is surveying the grounds in a sparkly red Bronco. I remark on all the changes since my last visit. "We just have a limited amount of space," he says. "All we can do is keep on redoing it."

"I guess you could go vertical," I say, flaunting my big-city real estate wiles.

Schafer shakes his head. "People won't go vertical. Our T-shirt shop is two stories, but it's deceptive; you can't tell till you're already inside. No, you can't get people to climb stairs. That's why every room in the motel is on the first floor."

The principle is simple, but I am impressed by the fact that Schafer resists the temptation to violate it; it would be so easy to double capacity by adding a second story. But then SOB would be perceived as less tourist-friendly, and people might shy away, knowing they cannot count on a ground-floor experience anymore.

Carolyn tells me that Schafer is a distributor for Miller beer (his territory covers about 67 percent of the state), which furnishes a substantial portion of his assets. His son Richard is in charge of that operation. Schafer also runs Ace-Hi Advertising, which provides SOB's billboards and the big outdoor Pedro figures. Schafer conceives all the billboards himself. He used to refer to himself as a frustrated adman, but I suspect he is happier as Pedro's *padre* than he would be as Darrin Stevens.

We glide electrically onward, past the Rodeo Drive Shop. Carolyn tells me SOB installed this ritzy emporium in response to customers' requests for a place where they could buy classier, more substantial gifts than the cheap Taiwanese trinkets for which SOB is famous. I make a hasty reconnoiter inside, and indeed there are some substantial items—tawdry, unnecessary items, but quite high-priced nonetheless. It seems, however—and no doubt Schafer knows this better than anyone—that what people really want is a classier setting in which to buy the same old cheap trinkets. The big-ticket backdrop makes customers feel . . . expansive: "For you, my dear. A lobster-claw oven mitt. I bought it at the *Rodeo Drive Shop*."

We pull up at the SOB Motel, where I will be "working" behind the desk. The motel's distinctive features include a squadron of sombreroed young bellboys, known as Pedros, who guide you to your room, riding ahead of your car on bicycles, and an indoor recreation center, Pedro's Pleasure Dome.

I study the check-in procedure. The motel has 92 rooms at $29 each that are rented on a first-come, first-served basis, 152 reservable $42 rooms, and 24 suites. (SOB is famous throughout the South for its "heir-conditioned honeymoon suites," which are sometimes actually used by real newlyweds.) SOB stopped taking "guaranteed reservations" when the pernicious credit-card companies, especially American Express, refused to bill their customers for no-shows and unfairly charged SOB's account instead.

Although there's almost always a room available, by 5 P.M. today the motel is full, except for suites and reservations, which will be held until about eight-thirty. There are so many weary travelers out there, even the suites should be occupied tonight. Nonetheless, most tourists, especially those with European accents who think they are too smart to let these Americans (or are they Mexicans?) try to put one over on them, turn frosty and rude when told there are only suites available.

Answers to popular motel questions:

➤ They will not hassle somebody if there is a suspicion of there being more people in the room than were paid for. "It doesn't cost us any more for that extra person," says manager Randy Craft, "but we lose the cost of the room if they get mad and leave."

➤ Unmarried couples registering under separate names will not be condemned.

➤ If you steal less than five dollars' worth of stuff they will not pursue the matter.

➤ The three-dollar "room key" deposit for cash customers is actually to offset unpaid phone charges.

➤ BONUS TIP: If you want two rooms but only want to pay for one, initiate a loud domestic quarrel. Security is scared senseless of these, and will gladly offer a complimentary second room so that you might "cool out."

SOB's appeal is not lost on the show-biz firmament. Celebrity guests have included George Jones, Bert Parks, even tiny little Radar O'Reilly. When Parks was here, the electricity had gone out and they were using candlelight, so nobody recognized him. "Don't you know who I *am?*" the legendary emcee finally exploded.

SOB keeps on file your sign-in paperwork (known as the folio) for five years, in order, for example, to provide evidence for police investigations. Craft shows me documents from a recent drug case where the prosecutors requested a phone log of the defendant. "Miami Vice"-y!

Craft tells me it's time for him to take a tour of the grounds—in a golf cart (!). He's from North Myrtle Beach, an hour east, and yes, he knows Vanna White. (There's a welcoming sign at the city limits identifying it as her hometown.) We cruise the motel grounds looking for things out of the ordinary, but all is disappointingly tranquil in the drowsy late-afternoon heat.

Saturday night, as Elton John once sang, is all right for fighting (With whom? His dippy lyricist? His hair-plug specialist?), and I'm expecting some action as I prepare to ride shotgun with Allan Rogers of the SOB security patrol. We will be on four wheels for the entire shift—in a car, not an electric cart, but we will be getting paid to cruise nonetheless.

Despite their meager 135-acre jurisdiction, security usually has two cars patrolling SOB at all times. The patrolmen, outfitted like state troopers, point out that they defy the stereotypically clownish image of security guards. One reason is the isolation; it would take Dillon police ten to twelve minutes to get here, so the SOB squad must be prepared to dispatch perpetrators themselves. Schafer misses a trick here by not accoutering his security force like sadistic, gun-happy Mexican *policía*—the type who would slice your eyelids off for littering—but I suppose he has his reasons.

Although only in his early twenties, Allan is a peacemaker: his mandate is not to slam citizens into walls, but to keep things running smoothly, to be a deterrent presence. Not that SOB is crime-free, he tells me, as we pass the gas station. People have tried to tank up without paying, he says. Once they leave the premises, however, crooks become the concern of the highway patrol. I ask how often SOB gets stung by a "gas and dash."

"Oh, every couple months or so," he replies.

I begin to worry that maybe SOB isn't going to be the hotbed of Southern rowdies I'd anticipated.

Just then, a call from one of the gift shops: someone is trying to pass a counterfeit ten-dollar bill. Allan rendezvouses with another guard at the shop and they grill the suspects, a clean-cut young couple with children. The guards confiscate the inauthentic bill. The family, obviously innocent victims, are released.

Allan tells me the bulk of the serious calls involve video-machine break-ins and fights at the saloon. Saloon brawls usually come on Friday nights—state law closes all bars at midnight on Saturday—and involve drunken, knife-wielding Lumbee Indians.

We see a plume of colored smoke rising from the parking lot of the convention center. Someone is setting off fireworks; in South Carolina, this is illegal on the same premises where you buy them. Allan is sympathetic. After all, the idea is to get people all excited about the great fireworks for sale here; what mortal could resist wanting to set some off after purchasing a trunkful? But what has Allan concerned is the vanload of partyers shooting off the fireworks. Dozens of empty beer cans clatter out the side door. He tells the celebrants to find an empty field a mile down the road if they want to use the fireworks, and to make sure—and here he gets stern—the driver stays away from the beer.

"Yesh shir, heesh not habbin' no beer hisshelf," vouches a tubby imbiber. We'll take his word for it, but Allan will especially keep an eye out for that van.

Unlike most Southern towns, where out-of-state plates are regarded with suspicion, at a traveler's outpost like SOB it's the cars with the local plates that signal misbehavior. If one is spotted on motel grounds at night, it is checked out. We behold none, however, and a disappointingly placid Saturday night ends with the isolated whimpers of mildly illegal firecrackers.

A call comes over the walkie-talkie: that "counterfeit" bill was legitimate, just an old, worn-smooth series 1934. Ha ha.

☞ Sunday

Before beginning a shift as a stock boy and cashier at one of the gift shops, I head for the clamorous pay phone next to that electronic smart aleck to check on things at home. (The phone in my motel room is rotary—I can't use my calling card.) The bedeviling little bugger plays his maddening theme song—whooor whoor woo woo woo woo woo woo woo—then cracks a sassy "Hey, where ya' goin'?" as I greet my girlfriend, Julie. "Who *is* that?" she asks of my intrusive neighbor.

As I explain, her other line rings, and Julie goes to answer it. She is gone quite some time, and I prepare some snappy repartee regarding the expense of a long-distance phone call. But Julie returns to inform me that my mother has been in a serious car crash in Chicago and is in intensive care—the other guy is dead. As my mind whirs at the tragedy, I do not shut out—as in point-of-view shots in movies where the protagonist is so wrapped up in some internal calamity that his background becomes a visual and audio blur—my surroundings. If anything, they intensify. The little cretin is still at it: "Hey, what's your name? Hey! Whooor whoor woo woo woo woo woo . . . "

I try to call the hospital, but the cheapo telephone screws up as I try to access MCI: "Please deposit . . . nine dollars and ninety-five cents. . . . Please deposit . . . nine dollars and ninety-five cents. . . . " Even for such an important call, this seems like a lot of change to scrounge up. After many attempts, I am able to get through, but I learn nothing of Mom's condition.

Besides her uncertain health, my greatest worry is that this quest might degenerate into some shameless fling at cheap sentiment, like the contemptible way a dead mother is crowbarred into *Bright Lights, Big City*. Since I can't do anything, can't even learn anything, about my mother, there is no reason not to proceed with the quest.

I go meet Lois Ann Miller, the manager of Mexico Shop West,

the largest of the gift shops. There's nothing like being surrounded by America's finest array of souvenirs to soothe one's tattered nerves. Over a thousand sales are rung up on an average day; the mean purchase is around ten dollars. This may not seem like much, but remember what is sold here: ashtrays, key rings, squeeze mugs, shot glasses, ceramic animals from Southeast Asia, Mike Tyson and Margaret Thatcher boxing puppets, novelty items based on bad puns.

Of course, for many this is a rare opportunity to purchase gifts from exotic lands. In fact, in 1958 the *Dillon Herald*, in an article on the Mexico Shop, called the establishment "not just a collection of trinkets, but an educational experience equivalent to touring Latin America for a month."

The clerks work on commission, receiving 1 percent of all sales; cashiers receive ½ percent. Although, as I think I mentioned, the merchandise is basically soulless "junque" (as Pedro says), the employees treat customers as respectfully as at a small-town J. C. Penney's. They will attentively field ridiculous questions about absurd products as if hosting a garage sale of family heirlooms.

It strikes me how ironic it is that at this place, which is considered so tacky, so trashy, things are run so much better, the help is so much less snooty, than at respectable tourist stops, like Santa Fe art galleries, Frank Lloyd Wright erections, or national parks where rangers ooze contempt and regard you as a wildlife-boofing arsonist. As roadside photographer extraordinaire John Margolies says, the only thing that's tacky is to be boring. *That* SOB is *not*.

I spend some time clerking, which consists of roaming the floor and returning mislaid merchandise to its proper place. It's a Sisyphean (a word that is almost as fun to use as "erection," as in "Frank Lloyd Wright erection") task: as I replace a rubber snake in its bin, I spot at least two customers mislaying merchandise. The will to bear novelty items, transport them, zombielike, then deposit them just anywhere must be powerful indeed, I muse. (You know what other word makes me crack up? "Cunningness.")

I do some cashiering, an agreeable task despite the steady business. Many customers are mind-boggled, having just arrived at SOB, and are cheerfully inquisitive. ("What the hell kind of place *is* this?" they might say, for example.) The other cashiers, who chat away amiably and seem to enjoy their work, answer my favorite question: "What celebrities have been here?"

"[Country-music 'artist'] T. G. Sheppard stopped here," says one. Another brightens. "[Country-music 'artist'] Lee Greenwood bought a hat at the Little Mexico Shop. I recognized him and said, 'Aren't you Lee Greenwood?' He tipped his hat, then tipped it again when he was leaving. I almost died."

"Oh, and [rock & roll 'douchebag'] David Lee Roth bought fireworks here last summer. But he was in disguise."

In an interior room in the store, behind painted glass, is the Dirty Old Man Shop, which sells naughty items and souvenirs, including personal vibrators, bachelor-party favors, and a series of slim pamphlets—marked down to forty-nine cents—featuring grainy black-and-white photos of ugly women with humongous, floppy breasts. The titles, which include "Bizarre Sex" and "The French Way," vary, but the content of each is the same: grainy black-and-white photos of ugly women with humongous, floppy breasts. Truckers please note.

It's time for my Sunday afternoon bingo game. I am embarrassed when I arrive at the hall, because Carolyn has arranged for me to receive special attention. The hair on the moles of the other players rises like that of threatened dogs; they sniff me suspiciously. It could be, as Pedro says, beeg trouble eef I ween game today.

I have my Dab 'n Glo Fluorescent Bingo Marker. I have my sheets of bingo cards. I have my Diet Coke. I have two floor runners supervising me to ensure I mark off all I have coming to me.

Each sheet has nine bingo cards on it; you use a different sheet each game. Some players buy two or even three stacks of sheets. The game requires a certain adeptness at spotting numbers quickly, for the pace is pretty brisk, but the main talent needed is the ability to stay alert and not daydream in the middle of a game—a deficiency in this trait is my proverbial Achilles tendon. An electronic board keeps track of all the numbers called, but after a reverie of unknown duration, it's nearly impossible to catch up.

When "Bingo!" is called, it has to be verified, but the crowd is so hardcore they will trash their sheets as soon as the shout is heard. I wonder if they would rely on a stranger's competence, and consider shouting "Bingo!" just to see if everyone would crumple their sheets, then have to dig them out of the garbage and fight over whose is whose when I stop fooling around and say, "Ha, ha—just kidding." I ask one of the runners, "I know you're just supposed to shout, 'Bingo!' but what do the really cool players do? Is there a cool way to announce it?"

She is perplexed. "No," she says sweetly, "you just jump up and shout, 'Bingo!' "

I decide to wait on my funny prank. My cards are performing

miserably. I watch the winners. They are happy, sure—payoffs range from $150 to $499, in a flashy shower of cash—but there is no game-show exultation. This crowd plays so often, they take a long-run view. A win is to be expected every X number of games.

I win nothing. First my mom, now this. I call the hospital: the injuries are severe but she will recover. She is all doped up on morphine and sounds like a wino, or that gal who tried to sell me dance lessons at Arthur Murray's. Any phone conversation seems extraordinary from the heart of Pedroland, but this one seems weighted by tons of goofy irony.

☞ M o n d a y

Fort Pedro, the fireworks store, has been open round the clock all weekend, and business is fantastic. I check in for some spine-tingling stock-boy action, and there are labor opportunities aplenty. I ask manager Ken Campbell what his biggest seller is. He shrugs; although M-70s are flying out of the store, at this time of year people are grabbing and buying everything, often without even knowing what they've got. I restock the shelves. It's true; *everything*, even odd-shaped packages of inscrutable contents, has been depleted. I dump huge piles into the bins, replenishing the huge piles that were dumped there just yesterday.

Fireworks are extremely profitable: Schafer estimates they account for one-sixth of SOB's total annual sales of $30 million. Most of the inventory comes from China, which, this July 4, is an unsettled foreign land indeed. This year's stock was ordered and shipped long ago, but next year's Independence Day celebration might prove the quietest ever. It's hard to imagine, but the turmoil in China could very well have a devastating impact on a self-contained little Mexican-ish wonderland in rural Carolina. Let's hope, for Pedro's sake, the golden door to the Land of the Eggroll reopens soon.

Speaking of ugly confrontations, a twisted sort of Hatfield-McCoy feud exists here at SOB. Although Schafer has tried to buy up all the land surrounding his domain, a tiny patch, near the entrance, remains in the defiant hands of another, who rents the space to a shameless roadside rival. The first place an average traveler succumbing to SOB's relentless exhortations will encounter is Jabs Fireworks, a small shack possessing a very bright and conspicuous sign. It sure looks SOB-like, and if you don't know better you might tool in to Jabs, procure bags of fireworks, get back on I-95, and think you have been to South of the Border. But you haven't, because Jabs parasitically feeds off SOB's fame, like the motley attractions that have sprung up near Disney World, in Kissimmee and Orlando, Florida.

The name Jabs is appropriate, because, although he won't admit it, the store's infuriating presence is like a sharp jab in the ribs to a control master like Schafer. Schafer countered by opening a mini-store, Lo-Bo's Fireworks, on his property, barely twenty feet from Jabs, trying to recapture some of Fort Pedro's stolen business. Although Fort Pedro is by far the largest and most commodious of SOB's fireworks emporiums, Jabs and Lo-Bo's, being located right at the entrance, do astonishing business. This is explained, I surmise, by the fact that fireworks, being illegal in so many states, have a furtive appeal. Customers feel they are circumventing the system by crossing the border and stocking up, so they want to get in and out quickly.

My stint at Fort Pedro is uneventful, as I am incapable of answering customers' questions about products that are extolled on the package in Asian Mondo English. All I can do is assure them of a thrilling, potentially dismembering adventure with each and every item—why, just look at that scary dragon on the box! Several people whom I don't recognize greet me; they remember me from the bingo game yesterday. Wasn't I that guy who had all the runners pointing at his card and telling him to mark off the numbers? It's a real taste of small-town life. Here, if you merely play a game of bingo you become an indelible part of the community. Let me out!

My last excursion at SOB will be a tour on the afternoon shift with Charles Weatherford, the chief of the SOB police. The criminal element at SOB has been dormant all weekend, so Weatherford regales me with classic cop stories. He tells me that many a man on the run —including a pair of escaped convicts in prison garb—has paused here and tried to blend in with the crowd, so the highway patrol keeps him informed of suspects who might be passing through. The escaped cons, in fact, were captured here, skulking around in their jailhouse clothes. (If only they had stopped at Pedro's T-shirt shop for a MY WIFE SAID IT WAS EITHER FISHING OR HER—I'M GONNA MISS HER shirt.)

Passing the Sombrero Tower, I wonder if anyone has ever taken a swan dive from the hat rim. No, he says, but once a lady threatened to. What troubles the chief about the tower is that it would make a dandy sniper's nest; this could create mayhem on a crowded summer day.

A cheerful, red-faced pappy jogs up to the patrol car, huffing and occasionally puffing. "Where's that Dirty Ol' Man Shop?" he says with a leer. The chief points him to the Mexico Shop West. The guy leans on the driver's window, grinning. "Thought maybe it was gone," he says. "Haven't been there in a few years."

"Well," says the chief, "it's over there."

The man grows more demented every moment. "Yeah, great, the Dirty Ol' Man Shop. You been there?" The chief smiles sourly and drives off.

I check out with less than five dollars' worth of SOB Motel furnishings and speed home in a pissy drizzle. It would make Ripley's for sure if, two days after Mom, I were to get wrecked up on the drive home. Life is generally un-Ripleyish, however, and this comforts me. Sure enough—wouldn't you know it?—I arrive back home safely.

COMPUTATION OF QUEST QUOTIENT

$$QQ = \frac{(M_d/100 + M_f/1000 + P/10 + L/5 + (I \times 10) + D + T) \times DA}{(F/10) + (\$/100) + 1}$$

Mileage driven: M_d = 1210
Mileage flown: M_f = 0
Phone calls: P = 4
Letters: L = 1
Intimacies: I = 0
Drop Dead factor: D = 0
Days spent: T = 5

Difficulty-Aggravation multiplier: DA = 3

Failure rate: F = 0
Cost: $\$$ = 350

QUEST QUOTIENT = 11.8

☞ *Analysis:*

Low Difficulty factor—Mr. Schafer is an affable host. . . . But unexpectedly high Aggravation factor—thanks to news of Mother's car accident as well as dementia with telephone— saves day (and DA!).

USA
25
Freddie Prinze

The Freddie Prinze Commemorative Stamp

he tragedy of the short, turbulent life of Freddie Prinze, nee Pruetzel, was perhaps best expressed by Jose Feliciano in his theme song for Freddie's monster hit sitcom, "Chico and the Man":

"Oh, Chico/
Etc."

Who knows how far America's greatest Hunga-rican (half Hun-garian, half Puerto Rican) comedian would have gone had he not killed himself at the age of twenty-two: Vegas? Tahoe? Reno? Atlantic City? Answer: No one.

The lessons of Freddie's textbook "too much, too soon" career become less legible upon the chalkboards of history each year. "Chico and the Man" reruns, though urgent and compelling on comedic merit, tell us little of the real Freddie, the tortured soul who both epitomized the American Dream and buckled under its relentless pressures. Surely there must be some vehicle to remember Freddie, the Great American—some commemoration that will touch our daily lives without taxing our patience.

I am flipping through the photo section of *The Freddie Prinze Story*, written by Freddie's mother, Maria, and admiring Freddie's many fashion statements: the Qiana shirts, the frilly tuxes, the "swingin' bachelor" turtleneck sweaters. It occurs to me that Freddie had as much an impact on the style of the mid-'70s as did Elvis Presley twenty years earlier. If you think about it, the ubiquitous influence of Freddie Prinze made him, in fact, the Elvis of the '70s, while his rebelliousness and life span evoked that of the other major '50s icon, James Dean. Freddie, indeed, was a "twofer."

Over the radio comes a report about a group of Elvis enthusiasts who are lobbying for a postage stamp honoring their King. My blood boils. Where is *my* generation? Are we all too busy worrying about the pinging in our BMWs or whether we should get rid of our record albums and switch to CD to stand up and say, "Hey, what about *our* hero, Freddie Prinze? What about *him?*" Instead of honoring a great American who let himself become irrelevant, why not honor a great American *who hadn't yet become relevant?*

My course is fixed. I will chair the Freddie Prinze Stamp Advisory Committee.

I write a letter to the Citizens Stamp Advisory Committee in Washington, which meets regularly to decide on who or what will be honored in stamp. (The one notable member of the committee is Digger Phelps, the coach of Notre Dame's basketball team.) The only restrictions are that nonpresidential honorees must be ten years deceased—check—and must be of national significance—double check. I present what I consider to be a strong case for Freddie, not the least of which is the fact that few Americans of Hispanic descent have been honored on postage stamps, let alone those who anybody's ever heard of. After several weeks, it is apparent I will receive no response. Or else it has been lost in the mail.

The next task is to rally support for the stamp. My friends at *Spy* magazine, Freddie fanatics one and all, produce for me a stunning mock-up of the Freddie Prinze commemorative in gaudy, Qiana-ish tones of purple and blue. They also supply stationery and a mail drop. I send a repro of the stamp, along with a letter and a blank petition form, to several dozen national Hispanic organizations, from the Congressional Hispanic Caucus to the Alliance of Latin Artistes Society to the American Association of Hispanic CPAs. I ask each organization to go on record in support of the stamp and to circulate petitions.

I send a similar letter to various celebrities who I would like to have in the pro-Freddie-stamp camp: David "Nobody Ever Sees You Eat Tunafish" Brenner and Tony "Knock Three Times" Orlando, who were pals of Freddie; Mike "Not Michael" Douglas, who had Freddie as a cohost on his show for an entire unforgettable week; Frank "Bad, Bad Leroy Brown" Sinatra and Milton "Did I Mention That I Have a Really Big Dick?" Berle, presidents of the Friars Club East and West, "respectively"; Jose "Can You See" Feliciano, who wrote and sang "Chico" 's stirring theme song; Geraldo "Jerry Rivers—Who's He?" Rivera, who kind of resembles Freddie and who I figure will want to get in on anything underscoring his alleged ethnicity; Charo ("Coochie-Coochie"), America's most prominent Latina; Johnny "Funny Nickname" Carson, who was almost singlehandedly responsible for Freddie's meteoric rise, and therefore for his death; Zsa Zsa "Another Funny Nickname" Gabor, America's most prominent Hungarian; and Kathryn L. Hutchinson, president of the Julio Iglesias Fan Club.

Spy, in honor of a man whose work influenced so many, offers me a private phone line to field the many calls that will soon be forthcoming. The line had been used previously for a recording that would reveal certain information related to a "game" that was contained in a recent issue of the magazine. I am assured that the game is now over, and that only legitimate Freddie Heads will be calling this number.

Three days after sending the letter, I've got fifteen messages on the Freddie Prinze Stamp Advisory Committee's answering machine. Loooooking goood! All, however, are from wise-guy and -gal *Spy* readers expecting information about that game. Their natural reaction is not to say, "Oh, I guess the game is over," but to try to make sick jokes about our Hunga-rican Hero. One clown called back six times, each time trying to be funnier than the last. E.g., "Freddie's dead, that's what I said. If you want to be a stamp, why?—'cause Freddie's on the corner now." (This is a clever—not—reworking of the lyrics to Curtis Mayfield's "Freddie's Dead," from *Superfly*.)

The pattern continues for several weeks: many messages, none pertaining to the Freddie Prinze stamp, most maligning the delightful comic. Many mailings are being returned to the FPSAC: about a third of the Latino organizations have dissolved or moved with no forwarding address in the two years since the directory from which I obtained their names was published. After about six weeks, I still haven't heard from a *single one* of the organizations, nor have I heard from one celebrity, not even Geraldo. Over fifty mailings, not one response. How soon they forget!

It's time to move into Phase 3. I will try to get oral support from some of those to whom I sent the mailing, then incorporate these into a press release I will send to every major newspaper and magazine in the country.

I begin by phoning the ethnic organizations:

Congressional Hispanic Caucus: Chaired by Congressman from Puerto Rico. I call day after he is unseated in election. Bad time to call. "Never received letter."

Puerto Rican Association for Community Affairs: Never heard of Freddie. "Never received letter."

Hispanic Society of America: Freddie is "vaguely familiar." Also, "Never got letter. Will call you back." Didn't.

President of Hungary: "Call consulate." I call consulate. "Talk to the cultural events consul." "Okay." "He's out of the country."

Association of Hispanic Arts: Unpleasant lady who *did* receive letter: "We're not in the position to endorse or not endorse anything regarding the government." Having grant trouble, unpleasant lady?

The celebrities were no more forthcoming:

Tony Orlando: "He did receive your letter. He seems not to have a comment."

Johnny, Charo, Mike Douglas, Zsa Zsa, Sinatra, Berle, Geraldo:
    "Will call back, tee-hee-hee."
Feliciano, Brenner: Out of town. For a long time. If you get my mean-
    ing.

I do receive the blessings of two Hispanic organizations, though
I'm sure neither has a clue as to who Freddie Prinze is—not that I
care. I use these as the centerpiece of a release entitled "Freddie
Prinze Stamp Receives Support from Famous Humorists and Latino
Organizations." I decide to call myself Juan, in case anybody wants
to interview me. The release, along with the stamp, is mailed to
almost one hundred print-media outlets. Let the avalanche begin!

Two weeks later I have received but one call. Only one publication sees fit to cover this honorable mission. And that publication
is . . . *Harper's!* Yikes! It's certainly proving a lot easier to be ex-
cerpted and ridiculed in that magazine than to be published through
legitimate means. However, I am not about to turn down the one place
that is interested in my quest. I return the call and am grilled about
the Freddie Prinze Stamp Advisory Committee. How many members?
How are you funded? *Harper's,* smarting from the recent *Please
Stand By* debacle, is not about to be led down a garden path.

"Oh, we have about twenty members, but only a handful work in
our offices full time. You say you're from *Harper's Bazaar?*"

"No, *Harper's* magazine. You have offices!?"

"Well," I confess sheepishly, "just a few modest rooms. We have
a pretty small budget."

The *Harper's* guy is salivating so hard at our misguided energies
I'm afraid he'll short out the phone. "Do you have a color version of
the stamp?"

"Yes, indeed. It's quite lovely." I decide to play it a little cagey.
"But we're only sending them to places that will actually use them.
They're expensive."

Mr. *Harper's* Guy does not want to be accused of lack of enthusiasm. "Oh, we're *very* interested. It's just the sort of thing we would
run."

I send him a color copy of the stamp. Several days later he leaves
a message on the machine. He is chortling outright at the expense of
Freddie's memory, chortles he will soon regret. "Do you have a better
quality version of the stamp?" he asks. "We want to run it."

Heh, heh, heh.

The Freddie Prinze Stamp Advisory Committee does not end here, however. We will use our *Harper's* clip to lend us even more respectability. We will petition, perhaps even pester, the members of the Citizens Stamp Advisory Committee until we are satisfied.

SPORTS ANNOUNCER

The Fighting Irish need a bucket here with just ten seconds left on the —wait. There's someone on the court, pestering Coach Phelps. . . .

So, if, on a crisp December day in 1993 you are buying stamps at the post office, and you should find yourself eyeball to eyeball with Chico himself—buy a sheet or two. 'Cause remember—Freddie's dead.

COMPUTATION OF QUEST QUOTIENT

$$QQ = \frac{(M_d/100 + M_f/1000 + P/10 + L/5 + (I \times 10) + D + T) \times DA}{(F/10) + (\$/100) + 1}$$

Mileage driven: $M_d = 0$
Mileage flown: $M_f = 0$
Phone calls: $P = 70$
Letters: $L = 160/5 = 32$
Intimacies: $I = 0$
Drop Dead factor: $D = 10 + 148/10 = 24.8$
Days spent: $T = 7$

Difficulty-Aggravation multiplier: $DA = 4$

Failure rate: $F = 90$
Cost: $\$ = 120$

QUEST QUOTIENT = 16.1

☞ *Analysis:*

Drop Dead factor needs to be adjusted for pure apathy. Only a handful of people were actively in favor of my ceasing to exist, while most simply ignored me. So I adjusted the apathetic contingent by dividing that number, 148, by 10. . . . Similarly, Letters factor is deceptive, since many were mass-produced. I reduced letters count by a factor of 5 to compensate. . . . Failure rate based solely on goal of getting stamp approved would be 100 percent. But since point of quest was also to get others involved, and since Harper's unwittingly did such, I award myself 10 percent success rate. . . . DA multiplier reflects challenge of convincing a committee that routinely honors woodchucks and tricycles to consider a stamp for a TV star who took drugs.

THE HELL WITH 'EM . . .

Afterword: Abandoned Quests

And that's it for American Quest. *Feel like you're missing something—like about ten quests? I have a good explanation: my homework fell in a sewer.*

If you're "pro-choice,"

you'll be happy to learn that all of my aborted quests were self-determined. There wasn't one instance where some goon, by saying "NO!," was able to terminate a quest. On the other hand, a few quests were aborted in anticipation of a goon.

Quests were abandoned mostly because they turned out, once I began, not to be very interesting; they didn't have any "twist" to them. For instance, Play the Great Miniature Golf Courses might be appealing if I were to tour with, say, a midget, or were to hire local midgets to play with me, but without this garnish it's uninspired. For your information, so *you* can go do it, the best miniature golf courses in America, chosen with the help of John Margolies, coauthor of *Miniature Golf*, are, in geographical order:

➤ Castle Amusement Park Golf, Riverside and Fountain Valley, California
➤ Valley View, Great Falls, Montana
➤ Congo River Golf and Exploration Company, Kenosha, Wisconsin
➤ Tower T, South St. Louis, Missouri
➤ Sir Goony Golf, Chattanooga, Tennessee
➤ Plantation Falls Legendary Golf, Hilton Head Island, South Carolina
➤ Wacky Golf, Myrtle Beach, South Carolina
➤ Gorilla Country Minigolf, Atlantic Beach, North Carolina
➤ Old Pro Minigolf, several courses, Ocean City, Maryland
➤ Hutsy Putsy, Deposit, New York
➤ Hot Diggity Dog, Rome, New York
➤ Salute to the USA Miniature Golf, Weirs Beach, New Hampshire

The Great American Handshake seemed to tread the same ground as the Ten Kiss quest, so I dumped it. My five G.A.'s are:

➤ Chuck Berry (he would be real mean to me for sure)
➤ Hugh Hefner (in "the Grotto")
➤ Little Jessica McClure (with me standing on the metal cap over her Memorial Pit)
➤ Ralph Nader (with him wearing a fish tie, I had hoped)
➤ J. D. Salinger (asking him to sign a copy of *The Lives of John Lennon*)

The Coolest Places to Drive quest wasn't much "to write home about," so I took an "El Paso" on it. The cool places are:

➤ Bonneville Salt Flats, Utah (would attempt land-speed record here)
➤ Chandelier Drive-Thru Tree, Legget, California
➤ Chesapeake Bay Bridge/Tunnel, Maryland-Virginia (longest on earth)
➤ Confusion Hill, Lake Wales, Florida (cars roll uphill)
➤ Dike Bridge, Chappaquiddick, Massachusetts (a.k.a. Ted Kennedy Bummer Bridge; turns out it's rotting—not even pedestrians can go on it)
➤ Indy 500 Track, Indianapolis, Indiana
➤ James Dean's Death Route, from L.A. to Cholame, California
➤ Snake Alley, Burlington, Iowa (twisty, and in Iowa)

The Week in Breezewood, Town of Motels quest evolved into July 4 Weekend at South of the Border—an upgrade, be assured. The Kill Bigfoot quest—I don't want to encourage that sort of thing. Drive a Monster Truck over a Japanese Car? Great idea, but who's going to let me flip his $100,000 toy? Paint Pellet War posed too much liability and a probability of arrest—maybe for the sequel. Milk a Cow—pretty exciting, but I just let it slip away. Anything else not covered: hey, I ran out of money.

And what did I learn?

America is a "land of opportunity" indeed if you are willing to keep on pursuing your dream past the point of resistance . . . if you can appeal to your fellow man's "better nature," tapping his basic willingness to lend a helping hand, to pass on knowledge, wisdom, and lore . . . if you have a fresh vision that captures the imagination. And if you don't run out of money.

Index